BOLLINGEN SERIES XLI

the
CROWNE of all HOMERS WORCKES
Batrachomyomachia
Or the Battaile of Frogs and Mise.
His Hymn's — and — Epigrams
Translated according to y<sup>e</sup> Originall
By George Chapman.

London, Printed by Iohn Bill, his MAIESTIES Printer.

# CHAPMAN'S HOMERIC HYMNS
# AND OTHER HOMERICA

*Edited by*
ALLARDYCE NICOLL

*With a New Introduction by* STEPHEN SCULLY

BOLLINGEN SERIES XLI

PRINCETON UNIVERSITY PRESS

PRINCETON AND OXFORD

Published by Princeton University Press, 41 William Street,
Princeton, New Jersey 08540

In the United Kingdom: Princeton University Press, 6 Oxford Street,
Woodstock, Oxfordshire OX20 1TW

THE ORIGINAL EDITION, TITLED,

*CHAPMAN'S HOMER: THE ILIAD, THE ODYSSEY AND THE LESSER HOMERICA,*

WAS THE FORTY-FIRST IN A SERIES OF WORKS SPONSORED BY AND

PUBLISHED FOR BOLLINGEN FOUNDATION

Library of Congress Cataloging-in-Publication Data

Homeric hymns. English

Chapman's Homeric hymns and other Homerica / edited by Allardyce Nicoll ; with a
new introduction by Stephen Scully.

p. cm.

Includes bibliographical references.

ISBN 978-0-691-13675-2 (cloth : alk. paper)—ISBN 978-0-691-13676-9
(pbk. : alk. paper)   1. Hymns, Greek (Classical)—Translations into English.
2. Gods, Greek—Poetry.   I. Homer.   II. Chapman, George, 1559?—1634.
III. Nicoll, Allardyce, 1894–1976.   IV. Scully, Stephen, 1947–   V. Title.

PA4025.H8C48   2008

883′.0108—dc22      2008002024

British Library Cataloging-in-Publication Data is available

This book has been composed in Bell Typeface

Printed on acid-free paper. ∞

press.princeton.edu

Printed in the United States of America

1   3   5   7   9   10   8   6   4   2

# CONTENTS

*The* Homeric Hymns *and George Chapman's Translation*
*by Stephen Scully*                                                    1

*Editor's Introduction by Allardyce Nicoll*                           41

### The Crowne of all Homers Workes

To the Earle of Somerset                                              49
The Occasion of this Impos'd Crowne                                   54

AL THE HYMNES OF HOMER
An Hymne to Apollo                                                    57
A Hymne to Hermes                                                     83
A Hymne to Venus                                                     114
To the Same                                                          130
Bacchus, or The Pyrats                                               132
To Mars                                                              136
To Diana                                                             137
To Venus                                                             137
To Pallas                                                            138
To Juno                                                              138
To Ceres                                                             139
To the Mother of the Gods                                            139
To Lyon-Hearted Hercules                                             140
To Æsculapius                                                        140
To Castor and Pollux                                                 141
To Mercurie                                                          141
To Pan                                                               142
To Vulcan                                                            144
To Phœbus                                                            145

## Contents

To Neptune                                           145
To Jove                                              146
To Vesta                                             146
To the Muses and Apollo                              146
To Bacchus                                           147
To Diana                                             148
To Pallas                                            149
To Vesta and Mercurie                                150
To Earth the Mother of All                           151
To the Sun                                           152
To the Moone                                         153
To Castor and Pollux                                 154
To Men of Hospitalitie                               155

BATRACHOMYOMACHIA                                    157

CERTAINE EPIGRAMMS AND OTHER POEMS
OF HOMER
To Cuma                                              177
In His Returne, to Cuma                              177
Upon the Sepulcher of Midus                          177
Cuma, Refusing His Offer t'Eternise Their State      178
An Assaie of His Begunne Iliads                      179
To Thestor's Sonne                                   179
To Neptune                                           180
To the Cittie Erythræa                               180
To Mariners                                          180
The Pine                                             181
To Glaucus                                           181
Against the Samian Ministresse or Nunne              182
Written on the Counsaile Chamber                     182
The Fornace, Call'd in to Sing by Potters            182
Eiresione, or The Olive Branch                       184

## Contents

To Certaine Fisher-Boyes Pleasing Him with
    Ingenious Riddles             185
[Final Verses]             186

*Textual Notes*             191
*Commentary*             205
*Glossary*             213

# THE *HOMERIC HYMNS*
# AND GEORGE CHAPMAN'S TRANSLATION

*Stephen Scully*

George Chapman's Renaissance translation of the *Homeric Hymns* is its first rendering into English. Chapman's efforts stride with robust Shakespearean vigor and are a source of delight even for modern readers, both as poems in our tongue and as lovely stories of the Greek gods. The *Hymns* are a collection of thirty-three poems celebrating the gods and goddesses of the Greek Pantheon from Mother Earth, the Sun, and Moon to Zeus, his children, and his children's children. Though gathered under Homer's name, they are anonymous compositions, varying in length and excellence, the best having the concentration and splendor of Homer's own achievements. Like all Greek narrative poems, they are composed to entertain and enthrall even as they also reveal and honor a deity's deeds and powers. The many modern translations of these hymns testify to the pleasure they continue to bring both to students of Greek literature and to the general reader.

The *Hymns*, like the poems of Homer and Hesiod, are *epea*: epic songs in dactylic hexameter in an artificial poetic dialect. The hybrid collection, consisting of five long poems followed by twenty-nine short ones, vary in length from six hundred lines to just three. Yet, even within such variation, most of the poems exhibit a common form: (1) a formulaic opening identifies the god invoked and draws attention to the poem itself as a "beginning"; (2) the middle describes the god's birth or a telling attribute—in brief or at length; (3) a formulaic close bids farewell to the deity and again draws attention to the activity of singing as the composer indicates that he is about to move on to a new song. Often in this context the singer will ask the god to favor him over other poets in a competitive performance. To the best of our knowledge, the form is very old, invoking both a god and the performative nature of the song.

The date of the collection is uncertain. It appears to be late, compiled by scholars at the Library of Alexandria in the second century BCE. In all likelihood, the compilers were also the first to attribute the multiple hymns to Homer, although variations in diction, style, and geographical perspective indicate that most of the poems were composed at different times and places on the Asia Minor coast and the Greek mainland roughly between 675 and 450 BCE in the Archaic and Classical periods. The earliest extant references to the collection come from two very different authors in the first century BCE, the Epicurean teacher of philosophy Philodemus and the historian Diodorus Siculus, both of whom refer to "Homer in the hymns." Even though shared dialect, meter, and certain elements of style, especially in the splendor of the long narratives, might serve to remind later audiences of Homer, there were certainly many in this period who questioned the Homeric authorship of these poems. Such may be inferred from the scant reference to the collection in antiquity, including the surprising absence of any allusion to the *Hymns* in the ancient commentaries to the *Iliad* or *Odyssey*. But if not to Homer, the source of the poems could reasonably have been attributed to the Homeridae (Sons of Homer), a clan or school of rhapsodes in the Archaic and Classical periods who claimed descent from Homer; or, even more appropriately, attributed to Hesiod, Homer's contemporary, who in his *Theogony* and *Catalogue of Women* wrote about the gods, their births, attributes, and love affairs.

## *The* Hymns *and Chapman's Translation*

While the collection itself is late, the genre of these hymns almost certainly dates back to Homer's—and Hesiod's—time. When quoting from what he calls the *Hymn to Apollo* (with no reference to Homer), Thucydides refers to the song as a *prooimion*, or prelude (3.104). Plato uses the same term to describe a song that Socrates composes to Apollo while waiting in prison to drink the hemlock (*Phaedo* 60d). Pindar refers to something of the sort as a "prelude": "Just as the Homeridae, / singers of woven stories, very often / began with a *prooimion* from Zeus, so this man . . . " (*Nemean* 2.1–3). It was the custom in ancient recitations of long narrative epic about heroes, sometimes called an *oimê* (literally, a "path" or "poem"), to begin with a short poem to a god, a *pro-oimê*.[1] One Alexandrian librarian, Crates of Mallos by name, apparently knew of an edition of the *Iliad* which began with such a hymn: "Of the Muses I sing, and of Apollo, famous for his bow."[2] Evidence from Homer suggests such practices already existed in his time: when in the *Odyssey* the Phaeacian bard Demodocus "begins from the god" when about to sing the story of the Wooden Horse at Troy (*Od.* 8.499). If the *Homeric Hymns* are a residue of that tradition, it is easier to imagine that the shorter hymns in the collection offer a closer approximation of the Archaic "prelude" than do the long poems, even though Thucydides identifies the long *Hymn to Apollo* as a *prooimion*. Indeed, it is tempting to see

---

[1] For the use of *oimê* (path, course, road), a term found in Homer metaphorically to refer to an episode in epic poetry or even to the poem itself, in the *Odyssey*, see 8.74, 481, and 22.347. The term is not found in the *Iliad* or in Hesiod but appears in the *Homeric Hymn to Hermes* (#4) 451.

[2] For the reference to Crates of Mallos, a contemporary of the Homeric scholar and head of the Alexandrian Library, Aristarchus, see Martin West, ed. and tr., *Homeric Hymns, Homerica Apocrypha, Lives of Homer*. Loeb Classical Library 496 (Cambridge, Mass., 2003), p. 455. Compare *Homeric Hymn to the Muses and Apollo* #25.

in the five long poems at the beginning of the collection the evolution of an introductory poem into a new literary form.[3]

Even if the *Homeric Hymns* seem to have seen themselves as fulfilling that introductory function, they do *not* refer to themselves as *prooimia*. Rather, they call themselves "songs" (*aoidai*), and their composers "singers" (*aoidoi*) who "sing" (*aeidein*), also commonplace terms in Homer and Hesiod for epic singing. On rare occasions, the *Homeric Hymns* also identify themselves as "hymns" (*humnoi*), a term used rather vaguely once in Homer to refer to an after-dinner song and also found once in Hesiod. More pointed perhaps is the verb "to hymn" (*humnein*) [a song in praise of] a god, which is found in Hesiod and often in the *Homeric Hymns* but never in Homer.[4] It is from the verb that the noun came to specify a song in celebration of a god or goddess.

Even the shortest of the *Hymns*, a three-liner to Demeter, manages to convey much of the genre's formulaic structure:[5]

Of Demeter, golden-haired, revered goddess, I begin to sing,

[3] Hesiod's poetry also suggests a development of this form, although in a different direction. His *Theogony* and *Works and Days* are much longer than the longest of the *Homeric Hymns* but both open with a proem to a god and proceed to integrate those themes into the poem proper. The *Theogony* in its entirety could well be regarded as a hymn to Zeus, making it the longest and most elaborate of all such hymns from antiquity.

[4] For *hymnos*, see *Od.* 8.429, Hesiod's *Works and Days* 657 and 662 and fragment 357.2, and the *Homeric Hymn to Aphrodite* 5.293. In variant readings, two other hymns mention a "hymn" to follow (9.9 and 18.11). For singers (or the Muses) "hymning," see Hesiod's *Theogony* 11, 33, 37, 48, 51, 70, 101 and *Works and Days* 2; *h. Apoll.* 3.158 and 177–78, 190, 207; *h. Her.* 4.1; 9.1; *h. Helios* 31.1. Dionysus is called a god of "many hymns" (*polyhumnos*, 26.7).

[5] All translations from the Greek are my own and follow Martin West's Loeb text, *Homeric Hymns, Homerica Apocrypha, Lives of Homer*. To help the Greekless reader have a sense of the Greek line, I try to follow the Greek word order in the line and across the enjambment, if it occurs, but in no instance do I strive for a metrical arrangement.

both her and her daughter, the exceedingly beautiful
  Persephone.
Hail and farewell, goddess, and save this city here, and begin
  my song.          (*Homeric Hymn to Demeter* #13)

The lovely six-line *Homeric Hymn to Aphrodite* #10 conveys
almost all of the basic features:

The Cypriote-born Cytherea I shall sing, you who to mortals
give honeyed gifts. On her alluring face,
there is always a smile; an alluring bloom shines over it.
Hail and farewell, goddess, ruler of well-founded Salamis
And of all Cyprus: grant an alluring song.
And I shall remember both you and another song.
                    (*Homeric Hymn* to *Aphrodite* #10)

While the short poems can do little more than list a god's
spheres of influence or principal activity, the long songs mag-
nificently narrate the story of a god's birth or some other de-
fining episode in the deity's life, in a manner and style which
rivals Homer and Hesiod at their best.

Like Hesiod's *Theogony* and *Works and Days*, some of the
hymns, and especially the long ones, identify the honored
deity with a particular place. It is possible that these hymns
were performed in the context of religious festivals at those
places, even perhaps as part of ritual or cult. Those less tied to
place could have been performed in a variety of settings, rang-
ing from large formal affairs such as the poetic competitions
at public festivals or funeral games to more intimate gather-
ings at private banquets. In all settings, these songs may well
have been accompanied by dance.

When George Chapman in 1624 and near the end of his
literary life turned to translate these hymns, he had little or no
understanding of the peculiar properties of the *Homeric Hymns*.

Understanding them as Homeric poems, though devoid of the heroic pathos that so drew him to the *Iliad* and *Odyssey*, he took it upon himself to translate the hymns, along with the *Battaile of Frogs and Mise* and *Epigrams*, also by Homer he thought, as his final and crowning tribute to the one he considered the greatest of all poets. As he says about himself, with these poems translated, the work he was "borne to doe is done."[6] He published little else thereafter before he died in 1634. Chapman's renderings of the *Hymns* do not reach the majesty of his translations of the *Iliad* and *Odyssey* but even in these works we can witness his elegant command of *poesie*'s form and sound rarely matched in later renderings of Greek epic poetry. Consider his translation of the 3-line poem to Demeter (*To Ceres*) (#13):

> The Rich-hayr'd Ceres I assaie to sing;
> A Goddesse in whose Grace the naturall spring
> Of serious Majestie it selfe is seene;
> And of the wedded, yet in grace stil green,
> Proserpina, her Daughter, that displaies
> A Beautie casting every way her Raies.
> All Honor to thee, Goddesse! Keepe this Towne,
> And take thou chiefe charge of my song's Renoune!

Chapman was never one to resist embellishment or to strive for word-for-word translation, as his critics were wont to point out. His fondness for expansion and liberty of form can be only partly explained by his use of rhymed couplets. As he wrote in "The Preface to the Reader" to his 1611 translation of the *Iliads*: "if in some few places . . . , I be something paraphrasticall and faulty—is it justice . . . to drowne all the rest of my labour?" A truly faithful translator, for Chapman, was inspired by the "elegancie, height, intention and invention"

---

[6] Chapman's epigram at the end of *The Crowne of all Homers Workes*, line 1.

of the original poems and strove to "clothe and adorne them with words and such a stile and forme of Oration as are most apt for the language into which they are converted."[7]

In one instance, the composer of the long *Homeric Hymn to Apollo* (#3) deviates from the standard practice of anonymity and draws attention to himself as well as to the occasion for his singing. The Greek lines are worth translating because, since antiquity, many have taken them to be a description of Homer himself. As we shall, Chapman does as well. From the Greek:

> May now Apollo and his sister Atremis be gracious,
> and all you girls of Delos, welcome; about me—even in
>     future times—
> be mindful, if ever someone of men upon this earth,
> a long-suffering stranger coming here, inquires,
> "O Maidens, who is for you the best of all the singers
> having traveled here; which of them causes you the most
>     delight?"
> Then all of you need answer well in unison,
> "A blind man, who lives on rocky Chios,"
> of all the songs his are by far the best.
>
> (*h. Apoll.* 3.165–73)

Chapman translates:

> And you, O Delian Virgins, doe me grace,
> When any stranger of our earthie Race
> Whose restlesse life Affliction hath in chace
> Shall hither come and question you: "Who is,
> To your chaste eares, of choicest faculties
> In sacred Poesie, and with most right
> Is Author of your absolut'st delight?"

[7] From "The Preface to the Reader," drawn from lines 147–57.

[7]

*Stephen Scully*

> Ye shall your selves doe all the right ye can
> To answer for our Name: "The sightlesse man
> Of Stonie Chios. All whose Poems shall
> In all last Ages stand for Capitall."
>
> (*An Hymne to Apollo* 259–69)

Even with its convoluted syntax, Chapman's lines can still—four hundred years after their time—cause strangers much delight. But it is his identification with Homer that I wish here to stress. When he published his translation of the *Iliads* in 1611, he imagined Homer (filled with poetic fire but "outward, blind") praising the Englishman's efforts: "thou didst english me"; and of himself he said that the ancient master "brought stay to all my state; / That hee was Angell to me; Starre, and Fate."[8] Now when Chapman finds himself describing that "sightlesse man" after more than a quarter of a century of translating his works, we can almost see him looking in the glass and beholding himself as Homer: indeed on the engraved title page of this last volume the facial features of Homer and Chapman have an uncanny resemblance.

Both heights—and stumblings—of Chapman's translations can be seen in his version of the *Hymn to Venus* (#10), a rendering particularly gracious for its fluency, alliteration, enjambment, and end rhymes.

> To Cyprian Venus, still my verses vow,
> Who gifts as sweete as honey doth bestow
> On all Mortality; that ever smiles,
> And rules a face that all foes reconciles;
> Ever sustaining in her hand a Flowre

[8] From "Euthymia raptus" (1609), in Phyllis Brooks Bartlett, ed., *The Poems of George Chapman* (New York, 1962), p. 175, lines 36, 85 and 92–93, respectively. For Chapman inspired by Homer's soul, see George deF. Lord, *Homeric Renaissance: The Odyssey of George Chapman* (New Haven, 1956), pp. 16–17.

That all desire keepes ever in her Powre.
   Haile then, O Queene of well-built Salamine
And all the state that Cyprus doth confine!
Informe my song with that celestiall fire
That in thy beauties kindles all desire.
So shall my Muse for ever honour Thee,
And any other thou commend'st to Me.

In Chapman's expansion of three Greek words, "grant an al-
luring song," into a full rhyming couplet: "Informe my song
with that celestiall fire / That in thy beauties kindles all de-
sire," one can sense that he is addressing Venus in his own
voice, and masterfully. But earlier in the same passage, he had
stumbled into an awkward misunderstanding, rendering the
Greek "a lovely bloom runs over" Aphrodite's face as "Ever
sustaining in her hand a Flowre" that keeps alive her eternal
"Powre." Chapman loses his footing here because, turning his
back to the Greek text, he has his eye on the usually reli-
able word-for-word Latin gloss accompanying it. Trying to
make sense of the Latin *et amabilem fert florem*, "and she bears
a lovely flower," rather than the difficult Greek phrase, *eph'
himerton theei anthos*, Chapman gives us the banal image of
Venus forever holding a flower in her hand.

   Chapman also has little understanding of the form and occa-
sion of the ancient hymns. This is particularly evident from his
renderings of the formulaic opening and close of the *Homeric
Hymns*, lines which offer internal evidence that the hymns may
well have prefaced epic narration. Nine of the hymns explic-
itly open with, "I begin by singing of" (with a deity named),
drawing the audience's attention to the activity of performance
and to the fact that these hymns are "beginnings."[9] Chapman

---

[9] Cf. *Homeric Hymns* 2, 11, 13, 16, 22, 25, 26, 28, 31. Compare Hesiod's
*Theogony* 1.

takes great liberties especially with the formulaic close. In the Greek, ten of the hymns end with the formula "And I shall be mindful both of you and another song (*aoidê*),"[10] a repetition that one would never guess from Chapman's diverse endings:

> Both thee and others of th' Immortall state,
> My song shall memorize to endless date.
>
> (To Apollo, 3.836–37)

> So all salutes to Hermes that are due,
> Of whom, and all Gods, shall my Muse sing true.
>
> (To Hermes, 4.1010–11)

> So shall my Muse for ever honour thee,
> And (for thy sake) thy faire Posteritie.
>
> (To Venus, 6.31–32)

> And thus, all honor to the shepherd's King!
> For Sacrifice to Thee my Muse shall sing!
>
> (To Pan, 19.83–84)

> Haile then, Latona's faire-hayrd seede, and Jove's!
> My song shall ever call to Minde your Loves.
>
> (To Diana, 27.35–36)

These many variations show the enormous liberties Chapman took, especially in his later years, and his difficulty in understanding the genre he was translating.[11]

---

[10] Cf. *Homeric Hymns* 2, 3, 4, 6, 10, 19, 27, 28, 29, 30. Georgius Dartona's facing Latin translation in Spondanus's Greek text, *Homeri Quae Extant Omnia*, does not render the Greek in exactly the same way in every case but the variations are very slight.

[11] For other examples, see: "So shall my Muse for ever honour Thee, / And any other thou commend'st to Me" (To Venus, 10.11–12); "So I salute thee still; and still in Praise / Thy Fame, and others', shall my Memorie raise" (To Pallas, 28.25–26); "Yet not to you alone my vowes belong: / Others as well claime t'Homage of my song" (To Vesta and Mercurie, 29.29–30);

Two of the very late hymns explicitly say that the poet will next celebrate the famous deeds of heroes, characteristic of epic poetry. The way Chapman expands these references is in itself striking and suggestive of what he found meaningful in these hymns. In one instance, the Greek reads:

A)    having begun with you (Helios), I shall celebrate the
            race of mortal men,
        heroes whose deeds the gods revealed to mankind.
                                                        (31.18–19)

And the other reads:

B)    . . . having begun with you (Selene), I shall sing
        of the famous tales of mortal heroes, whose deeds
            singers,
        servants of the Muses, make famous from their
            enchanted mouths.                    (32.17–20)

Finding in these lines Homeric themes that forever stirred him—his fascination with half-God heroes, the model they provided for lesser mortals, the grip of sad death upon all mortals, including these half-god men, and poesie's sacred charge to celebrate them—Chapman embellishes these lines to read:

A)    . . . and then from Thee
        And all the race of complete Deitie

---

" . . . Sustaine a Minde / Propitious to me for my Praise, and give / (Answering my minds) my vows fit Meanes to live" (To Earth, 30.31–33). In a slight variant, another formula reads, "having begun with you (Aphrodite), I shall pass on to another *hymn*" (5.293) which Chapman translates: "My Muse, affecting first thy Fame to raise, / Shall make Transcension now to others' Praise" (To Venus, 5.486–87). The Spondanus text also prints this close for the *Hymn to Artemis* (Diana) (#9), line 8.

My song shall celebrate those halfe-God states
That yet sad death's condicion circulates,
And whose brave Acts the Gods shew men, that they
As brave may ayme at, since they can but die.

(To the Sun, 31.31–36)

B)  ... With thy grace begun,
My Muse shall forth and celebrate the praise
Of Men whose states the Deities did raise
To Semideities; whose deedes t'endlesse Date
Muse-lov'd and sweete-sung Poets celebrate.

(To the Moon, 32.24–28)

## GEORGE CHAPMAN, TRANSLATOR OF THE *ILIADS* AND *ODYSSES*

Homer's poesie, "in which Humanitie to her height is raisde, / Which all the world (yet none enough) hath praisde," shaped Chapman's literary life. Born in 1559, Chapman was the first to translate the *Iliad* and the *Odyssey* in their entirety into English and the first to introduce the *Batrachomyomachia* and the *Homeric Hymns* to an English-speaking audience. Without the *Iliad* in England's mother tongue, he felt his "kingdome's maine soule [was] maim'd."[12] In 1598 when he was almost thirty, Chapman published seven books (Bk. I, half of II, VII–XI) in thunderous fourteen-syllable rhymed couplets, and *Achilles' Shield* in a quieter iambic pentameter rhymed couplet. In 1600 he brought out the first twelve books in fourteeners, and on April 8, 1611,

---

[12] Both quotations from Chapman's dedicatory poem to his patron, "To the High Borne Prince of Men, Henrie Thrice," lines 39–40 and 34, respectively, published in his 1611 edition of the *Iliads*.

after translating the last twelve books in a frenzied eighteen months, he published the complete poem in that meter. The title page read:

THE ILIADS OF

HOMER

Prince of Poets.

*Neuer before in any lan-*

*guag truely translated.*

*With*

*a Comment uppon some of his chiefe*

*places;*

*Donne according to the Greeke*

*By Geo: Chapman.*

*At London printed for Nathaniell Butter.*

*William Hole sculp:*

Three years later, he brought out his *Odysses* (1614–15) in rapidly flowing, enjambed iambic pentameter rhymed couplets, admired by some for its more refined sensibility and seasoned hand than his robust *Iliads,* but it has its own excesses. Whereas Chapman's passionate *Iliads* was only 14,416 lines compared to Homer's text of roughly 15,700 lines, Chapman's *Odysses* was a whopping 16,663 lines compared to Homer's roughly 12,150 lines. About ten years later, Chapman published *The Crowne of all Homers Workes* (1624) including *Batrachomyomachia, or the Battaile of Frogs and Mise. His Hymn's—and—Epigrams Translated according to ye originall,* in decasyllabic rhymed couplets. One feels that Chapman, without heroic figures to animate his imagination, struggled to find his way with these latter poems. Rather than a climax, the last works represent something of a descent from his Olympus. Even so, his *Hymnes* are even more embellished than the *Odysses,* a total of 3,027 lines compared to 1,814 lines in the Greek.

Chapman's expansions are not due solely to his use of rhymed couplets and the shorter decasyllabic verse. As he aged, he felt ever more free to let Homer's poesie move through him and carry him to his own "true sence and height." "Word-for-word traductions," he complained, "lose / The free grace of their naturall Dialect / And shame their Authors with a forced Glose."[13] For literal renderings, Chapman advised his reader to pick up the Latin prose translations of Lorenzo Valla or Eobanus Hessus and convert them to verse. He also took delight in making fun of French and Italian verse translations with their polysyllabic end-rhymes concluding "in harsh Collision." In phrase of English, Chapman coos: "Our Monosyllables so kindly fall / And meete, opposde in rime, as they did kisse."[14]

In addition to his free paraphrase, critics with reason have chastised Chapman for his quirky English (often rich in invented words) and forced expressions midst the plain, natural, and most just—his entangled syntax leading one occasionally into difficult-to-escape-from thickets—and of course for his epithets. Coleridge was by no means alone when objecting to Chapman's "quaint epithets which he affects to render literally from the Greek, a language above all others 'blest in the marry marriage of sweet word,' and which in our language are mere printer's compound epithets—such as quaffed divine *joy-in-the-heart-of-man-infusing* wine to be one-word, because

---

[13] "To the Reader" (to be distinguished from "The Preface to the Reader," both in the 1611 *Iliad* edition), lines 120–22. The only English translation of the *Iliad* at this time was by Arthur Hall, *The Ten Books of Homers Iliades, translated out of the French* (1581), by Hugues Salel (1545), itself translated from Andreas Divus's Latin translation of 1537. Cf. Millar MacLure, *George Chapman: A Critical Study* (Toronto, 1966), p. 234.

[14] "To the Reader," lines 168–69.

one sweet mellifluous word expresses it in Homer."[15] As vulnerable as Chapman is to such criticism, his rendering of the Homeric epithet *also* deserves praise.

Even the first Renaissance translators of Homer into Latin stumbled over Homer's epithets, in no small measure because the Latin they imitated from Vergil's (and Ovid's) interwoven line was far from Homer's formulaic half-line cadences. Shaped by Vergilian and Ovidian poetics, these translations were doomed to appear clunky, graceless, and all too obviously "translationese" in their rendering of Homer's formulaic phrasing. Two early translations of the *Iliad* into Latin prose—the speeches of Book IX by Leonardo Bruni in the early 1400s and the whole poem by Valla in 1444—simply cut out the epithets. As Bruni explains: "I translated in the oratorical manner . . . leaving out epithets because they are the property of poets."[16] In English Chapman does much better. Even his quaint hyphenated compounds are almost invariably of his own design. So, for example, at *Hymne to Apollo* 3.21–22:

> All haile (O blest Latona!) to bring forth
> An issue of such All-out-shining worth,

Chapman creates a compound and an end-rhyme of his own choosing—again under the influence of the Latin gloss accompanying the Greek text. His "an issue of such All-out-shining worth" is closer in sense and structure to *praeclaros liberos* than to *aglaa tekna*, "the radiant children," of the original. Such

[15] George Whalley, ed., *The Collected Works of Samuel Taylor Coleridge* 12: II (= Marginalia II) (Princeton, 1984), p. 1119.

[16] Peter Thiermann ed., *Die Orationes Homeri des Leonardo Bruni Aretino: Kritische Edition*, Mnemosyne. Bibliotheca classica Batava. Supplementum 126 (Leiden, 1993), p. 66. Cf. Scully, "Homeric Epithets and Translation," *International Journal of the Classical Tradition* 11 (2004–2005), pp. 404–15.

examples abound. Even more to the point, *pace* Coleridge's claim, Chapman frequently ignores the epithets in the original and adds others where Homer has none. More often than not, these invented *nonhyphenated* epithets capture the flavor of the Greek more successfully than almost all other efforts in English: they are simple and straightforward, evoking an essential and generic quality of a noun, bringing it temporarily into focus, even energizing the line. Such verse is not Homer's but it is Homeric.

Three translations from the *Hymn to Aphrodite* (#5) illustrate the point: The first, by Diane Rayor, *The Homeric Hymns: A Translation, with Introduction and Notes* (Berkeley, 2004), is most literal:

> Seeing her, Anchises wondered, amazed
> at her beauty, her stature, her shining clothes!
> Her robe blazed past the radiance of fire,
> spiral bracelets and earrings shining like flower buds,
> with brilliant necklaces gracing her soft throat,
> like the moon shining on her soft breast,
> beautifully inlaid in gold, a marvel.
> Passion seized Anchises, face to face, he spoke to her . . .

Faithful to the Greek, there is a certain flow in Rayor's lines of three, four, or five beats but they lack rhythmical vitality and, as well, the connective tissue of vowel and consonant patterns. Compare Daryl Hine's translation (1971), republished by the University of Chicago Press and 2005 winner of the Landon Translation Prize from the Academy of American Poets:

> When he beheld her Anchises was filled with amazement
>     and wondered
> At her appearance and stature and also her shimmering
>     raiment,

Since she was wearing a mantle outshining in brightness the
   firelight,
Torques that were twisted in spirals and glittering
   flower-shaped earrings;
Necklaces lay on her delicate neck, of surpassing refinement,
Beautiful, golden and cunningly fashioned; a luster of
   moonlight
Shone round her delicate body; which was a great wonder to
   witness.
Longing laid hold on Anchises, who spoke to her something
   as follows: . . .

A master metricist, Hine manages what few can get away with
in English, Homer in dactylic hexameter. Meter drives the
narrative and is linked to a whole nervous system of caesura,
enjambment, vowel play, and alliteration. Though not particu-
larly illustrated in this example, Hine is often quite cavalier
with recurring epithets, sacrificing them for the contingencies
of meter and sound pattern. With the heroic couplet, Chapman
is even freer, extreme in adding ornaments but splendid in
flow, meter, texture, sound:

Anchises seeing her, all his senses were
With wonder stricken, and high-taken heeds
Both of her forme, brave stature, and rich weedes.
For, for a vaile, she shin'd in an Attire
That cast a radiance past the Ray of fire.
Beneath which wore she, guirt to her, a Gowne
Wrought all with growing-rose-budds, reaching downe
T'her slender smalls, which buskins did divine,
Such as taught Thetis' silver Feete to shine.
Her soft white neck rich Carquenets embrac't,
Bright, and with gold in all variety grac't,
That, to her brests let downe, lay there and shone

As, at her joyfull full, the rising Moone.
Her sight show'd miracles, Anchises' Heart
Love tooke into his hand, and made him part
With these high Salutations . . .

These three versions of the *Hymn to Aphrodite* 5.84–91 (Chapman, 136–51) illustrate the choices readers must inevitably make when selecting a translation. All of them take us only so far toward the original but at their best—"With Poesie to open Poesie"—they find their "naturall Dialect" and help enrich a "kingdome's maine soule."

Not all speak approvingly of Chapman's efforts. In 1875, for example, in an essay accompanying an edition of Chapman's writings, the poet A. C. Swinburne admired Chapman's "subtle and sleepless ingenuity" but criticized his inability to "resist the lure of any quaint or perverse illustration, . . . [of] the rough and barren byways of incongruous allusion, of unseasonable reflection or preposterous and grotesque symbolism. . . . For all his labours in the field of Greek translation, no poet was ever less of a Greek in style or spirit. He enters the serene temples and handles the holy vessels of Hellenic art with the stride and grasp of a high-handed and high-minded barbarian."[17] Today, we are less inclined to think of Greek temples, or thought, as serene, and better able to embrace the spirit and fluency of Elizabethan grandeur in Chapman's vocabulary, syntax, and cadences. His *Hymnes* are of interest to us today both for historical reasons as they are the first in our tongue and an admirable testament to a Renaissance effort to make Homer out of them. But they also are fascinating in and of themselves; Chapman's translations cannot rival many of the modern editions for their closeness to the Greek but we can still learn from him how to make Homer sound vital and vivid in English.

[17] Swinburne, *George Chapman: A Critical Essay* (London, 1875), pp. 3 and 6.

## *The* Hymns *and Chapman's Translation*

### Texts and Reception

By a curious twist of fate, the *Homeric Hymns* were more popular and widely known in Chapman's time than they were in antiquity. There are relatively few references to the collection in antiquity. In spite of their many geographical references and allusions to obscure events that would have aroused ancient pedants, there are no scholia for the *Homeric Hymns* themselves and few scholia to other authors refer to the *Hymns.*

From the Byzantine manuscripts, the *Hymns* entered the Renaissance either preserved as part of the Homeric corpus, along with the *Batrachomyomachia* and sixteen epigrams, or in company with other hymns from Callimachus, the Orphic tradition, or Proclus (mostly in the odd order of Orpheus, Proclus, Homer, Callimachus). With the Renaissance fascination for all things Homeric and mythological, the *Homeric Hymns* enjoyed a greater audience circa AD. 1500 CE than they had in their first seventeen hundred years. While the *Battle of Frogs and Mice* is scarcely read today, the *Hymns* have never been more popular than they are now. Close to ten translations in English alone are currently on the market, many of these published for the first time or reprinted within the past five years. The eloquent and unrivalled stories recounted in the long *Hymns* about many of Zeus's most prominent children account for their wide audience.[18] They are often read in courses alongside Homer or in conjunction with the *Theogony* as their stories of the gods charmingly complicate Hesiod's brilliant interpretation of Zeus's ascendancy to power and the stabilization of order on Olympus.

---

[18] These are Dionysus; Persephone, like her mother Demeter, in agony at Zeus's "marrying" her off to Hades; Apollo; Hermes; and Aphrodite, daughter of Zeus and Dione in *Hymn* #5 and in Homer but sea-born from Ouranus's severed genitals in Hesiod's *Theogony* and in *Hymns* #6 and 10.

By another quirk of fate, in Chapman's day the twenty-five extant manuscripts which included the *Homeric Hymns* began with the *Homeric Hymn to Apollo*. It would not be for another one hundred and fifty years, when Christian Friedrich Matthaei, a professor of Greek in Moscow, discovered in a barn outside Moscow in 1777 a manuscript from a different tradition, that scholars became aware that in the ancient collection a long *Hymn to Dionysus* (now in fragmentary form) began the volume, followed by the splendid *Hymn to Demeter*. Modern editions begin with these poems, numbering the *Hymn to Apollo* at the beginning of Chapman's translation as number three.

For his translations, George Chapman used the *Homeri Quae Extant Omnia. Ilias, Odyssea, Batrachomyomachia, Hymni, Poematia aliquot*, edited by Johannes Spondanus (Jean de Sponde), Basel, 1583, reprinted in 1606. This volume also contained Spondanus's Latin commentary and book-by-book argument for the *Iliad* and *Odyssey* which Chapman consulted actively; there were no such aids for the *Batrachomyomachia* or the *Hymni*. The volume included a facing Latin translation, which Chapman also consulted line by line, but he was by no means Greekless and blindly dependent upon the Latin, in spite of the claim of "a certaine envious Windfucker. That hovers up and downe, laboriously engrossing al the aire with his luxurious ambition and buzzing into every eare my detraction—affirming I turne Homer out of the Latin onely, etc.—that sets all his associates and the whole rabble of my maligners on their wings with him to beare about my empaire and poyson my reputation" ("The Preface to the Reader," 157–63 [1611]). As there was no indication to the contrary in Spondanus's text, Chapman thought these translations were by the editor but in fact they were reprints: the *Iliad* and *Odyssey* by Andreas Divus, the *Batrachomyomachia* by Aldus Manutius, and the *Hymni* by Georgius Dartona of Crete, published collectively in

*Homeri opera Latine ad verbum translata* (Venice, 1537). Franck Schoell's condemnation of Divus's translations for being "absurdly literal" and "greatly inferior Latin" misses the point.[19] These translations did not strive to be elegant or even good Latin but word-for-word glosses of the Greek, a feat possible in Latin but not in the less-inflected later European languages. Inevitably, they misconstrued a Greek phrase on occasion or in their severe constraints distorted coherence, but in general these renderings were remarkably successful for what they set out to be.

Chapman's translations remained popular until the end of the century but by the time of Alexander Pope's *Iliad* (1715–20) and *Odyssey* (1725–26), in refined end-stopped iambic pentameter couplets, they had become "totally neglected" according to Samuel Johnson. The tide turned with the English Romantics, due largely to the pull of Charles Lamb's enthusiastic endorsement. In 1808, his friend Samuel Taylor Coleridge sent a copy of Chapman's Homer to a young lady with a note saying that the translations with their "mighty faults counterpoised by mighty Beauties" were now "very scarce & valuable."[20] The availability of Chapman's translations appears to have changed within a decade. In 1616, Keats published "On First Looking into Chapman's Homer," and two years later Shelley, encouraged by his friend Thomas Hogg to read the *Homeric Hymns* ("miraculous effusions of genius" of "magical verses," in Hogg's words), began translating the *Hymns.* He began this project in

---

[19] Schoell, *Études sur l'humanisme continental en Angleterre à la fin de la Renaissance* (Paris, 1926), p. 152. *Pace* George deF. Lord, *Homeric Renaissance*, p. 24, Divus's lines are not "in hexameters" but in the nature of a gloss break at the end of the line in imitation of the Greek.

[20] For Johnson, see his *Lives of English Poets* (published in 1781), ed., G. B. Hill, (Oxford, 1905), vol. 3, p. 114; for Coleridge, see *The Collected Works*, vol. 12.II, p. 1119.

January of 1818 and by the end of the month had ordered a copy of Chapman's translation of them to arrive "if possible by tomorrows Coach."[21] By the end of the nineteenth century Chapman's Homer, including the *Hymns*, were reprinted or edited several times. The text printed here is from Allardyce Nicoll's excellent edition with introductions, textual notes, commentaries, and glossaries, *Chapman's Homer: the Iliad, the Odyssey, and the Lesser Homerica* (New York, 1956).

Coleridge praised "it" (presumably Chapman's *Odysses*, his favorite of the two poems), "as truly an original poem as the Faery Queen—it will give you small Idea of Homer; tho' yet a far truer one than from Pope's *Epigrams* or Cowper's cumbersome most anti-homeric *Miltoniad*—for Chapman writes & feels a Poet—as Homer might have written had he lived in England in the reign of Queen Elizabeth."[22] Matthew Arnold echoed these sentiments midcentury: "Chapman's style is not artificial and literary like Pope's nor his movement elaborate and self retarding like the Miltonic movement of Cowper.

---

[21] Shortly after this request, Shelley gave up on the project due to an eye illness. In that year, Shelley translated five *Hymns*: #28 and 30–33 (To Minerva, Earth, Sun, Moon, and Castor and Pollux) and the first fifty-eight lines in draft of #5 (To Venus), primarily in end-stopped heroic couplets; cf. Kelvin Everest and Geoffrey Matthews eds., *The Poems of Shelley*, vol. 2 (Harlow, 2000), pp. 338–39. In 1820 Shelley translated and freely expanded into playful *ottava rima* the *Hymn to Mercury* (#4). As this poem is about the invention of poetry and as one of Shelley's nicknames was Mercury, Shelley's rendering of Hermes' gift to Apollo: "I / Present thee with this music-flowing shell, / Knowing thou canst interrogate it well" (659–60) seems delightfully to evoke comparison between Shelley's name and his occupation; cf. Byron's characterization of his fellow poets as "brethren of the Shell," and Gary Farnell, "Rereading Shelley," *English Language Notes* 60 (1993): 634–36.

[22] By *Miltoniad* Coleridge means Cowper's translations of the *Iliad* and *Odyssey*, published in 1791.

He is plain-spoken, fresh, vigorous, and, to a certain degree, rapid; and all these are Homeric qualities." For Erza Pound in 1920, Chapman remained "the best English 'Homer.'"[23]

From his first days working on the *Iliads*, Chapman felt a yearning of the gods to come down from above and to engage with men ("downe from heaven Athena stoopt and shind / . . . and tooke / Achilles by the yellow curles," *Il.* 1.196–200) and a hero's capacity to rise up to meet the divine ("they were nimble wings, and made so light his spirit / That from the earth the princely captaine they tooke up to aire," *Il.* 19.372–73). Chapman is most at home in this vast cosmological exchange. In the rarer atmosphere of the *Hymnes*, he makes his way less easily but even here readers can find delight in the combination of Greek epic narrative and Chapman's English.

## THE ARRANGEMENT OF THE COLLECTION
### AND INDIVIDUAL *HYMNS*

The arrangement of the thirty-three hymns (thirty-one in Chapman) is not as arbitrary as it may at first appear. The collection begins with the long narrative poems, each several hundred lines in length, though these 5 hymns themselves do not conform to any discernible order and are not arranged in the chronological order in which they were composed. Judging from internal evidence, these songs were created for particular festivals or locales where the respective god was especially honored. The 28 short hymns have a certain internal logic, beginning with two longish hymns, one to Aphrodite (Venus),

---

[23] For Coleridge, see *The Collected Works*, vol. 12.II, pp. 1119–20; for Arnold's essay, see Arnold, *Essays, Literary and Critical* (London, 1907), p. 223; for Pound, see "Translators of Greek: Early Translations of Homer" (1920), in T. S. Eliot, ed., *Literary Essays of Ezra Pound* (Norfolk, Conn., 1954), p. 249.

the other to Dionysus (Bacchus) (in the Greek 21 and 59 lines, respectively; in Chapman, 32 and 103 lines, respectively). An anomalous poem to Ares (Mars), which Chapman admired, comes next, followed by 6 very short poems to goddesses, arranged from younger to older deities and culminating in a *Hymn to the Mother of the Gods* (#14, 6 lines long). After these come 9 very short poems to gods, again arranged from younger to older and culminating in a *Hymn to Zeus* (Jove) (#23, 4 lines long). Then appear 6 poems of varying length, framed by songs to Zeus's virgin sister, Hestia (Vesta) (#24 and #29), with songs to various of his children sandwiched in between. Three songs to very old gods follow: to the Earth, Mother of all (#30), Helios (Sun), and Selene (Moon) (#31 and #32). The hymns conclude with a song to the Dioscuri (Castor and Pollux), twins of a mortal woman, one of the sons fathered by Zeus, the other by Tyndareus, the king of Sparta. In this way, the collection begins and ends with songs to half-gods, made immortal—Dionysus and the Dioscuri, half-men not gripped by sad death. Seven hymns in this collection are to such figures: 3 to Dionysus (#1, #7, # 26); 2 to the Dioscuri (#17 and #33); 1 each to Heracles (Hercules) (#15) and to Asclepius (Aesculapius), fathered by Apollo from a mortal woman (#16). The collection ends with a song to Guests/Strangers (Xenoi), (Men of Hospitalitie in Chapman's translation [#34], though often not numbered; found in only some of the manuscripts).

Ignoring the arrangement of the collection, we may group the gods in the hymns into three sets:

I) Pre-Olympians:
   Mother of the Gods (#14)
   Earth, Mother of All (#30)

Helios (Sun) (#31)

Selene (Moon) (#32)

Aphrodite (Venus) (Hesiodic version, as in #6, #10)

II) The 12 canonical Olympians:

   a) Zeus and siblings:

     Zeus (Jove) (#23)

     Hestia (Vesta) (#24, #29)

     Demeter (Ceres) (#2, #13)

     Hera (Juno) (#12)

     Poseidon (Neptune) (#22)

     Not surprisingly, there is no hymn to Hades, Lord of the Underworld, Zeus's much-feared other brother, and rarely present on Olympus.

   b) Zeus's children (if one follows Homer and not Hesiod in thinking that Aphrodite is his daughter and Hephaestus his son):

     Athena (Pallas) (#11, #28)

     [Persephone (Proserpina) with Demeter (#2, #13)]

     Apollo (Phoebus) (#3, #21, #25 with the Muses)

     Artemis (Diana) (#9, #27)

     Aphrodite (Venus) (Homeric version, as in #5)

     Ares (Mars) (#8)

     Hephaestus (Vulcan) (#20), where his parentage is not specified, but in the *Hymn to Apollo*, Hera, enraged at Zeus for giving birth to Athena, gives birth to Hephaestus without male consort (3.317, in Chapman, *An Hymne to Apollo* 501–2)

     Hermes (Mercury) (#4, #18)

     Pan, Hermes' child (#19)

III) Children from a god and a mortal woman:

   a) immortal, Zeus's children:

     Dionysus (Bacchus) (#1, #7, #26)

     the Dioscuri (Castor and Pollux) (#17, #33)

      Heracles (Hercules) (#15)
    b) mortal(?), Apollo's child:
      Asclepius (Aesculapius) (#16)

As a collection, the hymns often complicate Hesiod's picture of the gods in the *Theogony*, even as they complement and confirm his understanding of an harmonious Olympus.

## THE HYMNS

The *Hymn to Apollo* (#3) (546 lines in Greek; 837 in Chapman). This is a remarkable tale of literary and textual interest. It was many years after Chapman's translation that scholars began to make sense of its tangle of narrative twists and turns. In two separate instances, it recounts the fear of the gods, and in particular the goddesses, at the arrival of this new god, first in the story of his birth on the island of Delos and then in the founding of his sanctuary at Delphi in mainland Greece. In both cases, instead of the young, powerful bow-god being a threat to Zeus and the new order of Olympus, Apollo proves to be the loyal son, eager to carry out the will of his father. As soon as he is born on Delos, he frees himself from his swaddling bonds and proclaims straightway: "The lyre and curved bow are dear to me, / and I shall prophesy to mortals Zeus's unerring plan" (3.131–32; Chapman, 195–97). The second tale records Apollo's struggles to clear the site of Delphi for his oracular home, a feat which in this telling entails the violent defeat of two female figures and Hera's monstrous son Typhaon. The three stories are so telescoped that the outer one about Apollo's hostile run-in with and eventual burying in a shower of stones the spring nymph Telphousa (244–76 and 375–87) frames the story of his violent slaying of the vicious female serpent, Pytho, who guards the spring near Delphi (277–304 and 356–74). Embedded within the Pytho story is a digression (305–55) about the birth of a male monster, Typhaon, whom Hera, in a rage at Zeus for giving birth to Athena, creates without consort and gives to Pytho to raise. In defeating Pytho, Apollo in effect slays Typhaon, though that is never said outright, and saves Zeus and the world at large from the destruction that Hera had desired.

Even in the Greek, the transitions in this intricately woven sequence of tales are abrupt and awkward, and especially so with the Typhaon digression, which drops into the narrative as if from outer space and similarly disappears without warning. It is remarkable that Chapman got through the sequence as well as he did, considering that he had no commentaries or other guides beside George Dartona's Latin translation facing his Greek text. Spondanus's Greek text does not make matters easy for Chapman when it prints Delphusa for Telphousa as if she were somehow Delphi. Chapman is aware that Pytho (Pythus in Chapman) is an alternate name for Delphi but for some reason he renders her as Dragonesse at 431–83a but as Pytho at 558b–92a. In Chapman the transitions between episodes are often blurred, occurring as they frequently do across a semi-colon in mid-line. In outline, a comparison of the three stories looks like this:

| *Greek Text* | *Chapman's Text* |
|---|---|
| Telphousa 244–76 | Delphusa 389–430 |
| Pytho 277–304 | Dragonesse 431–83a |
| Typhaon 305–55 | Typhon 483b–558a |
| Pytho 356–74 | Pytho 558b–92a |
| Telphousa 375–87 | Delphusa 592b–610 |

Chapman's translation of this hymn often seems labored but on occasion he approximates the "daring fiery Spirit" that Pope said animates the best of Chapman's *Iliads*.[24] Consider:

> The King Apollo, with an arrow, freed
> From his strong string, destroid the Dragonesse
> That Wonder nourisht, being of such excesse
> In size and horridnesse of monstrous shape,
> That on the forc'd earth she wrought many a rape,
> Many a spoile made on it, many an ill
> On crooke-hancht Herds brought, being impurpl'd still
> With blood of all sorts;                    (476–83a)

Long after Chapman's death, it was argued that the two episodes in the *Hymn* were originally separate poems. One poem concerned with Apollo's birth at Delos ended at line 178 (in Chapman, line 278);[25] it was performed at the Delian festival, while the other, of earlier date, concerned with the establishment of Delphi, was composed by a poet from central Greece. Variations in diction, formulaic usage, and geographical orientation in the two sections of the existing poem strongly support this view, but the shared themes and structure of the two parts also suggest that both poems were reworked, rather successfully, to interweave the separate pieces into a single, coherent poem. Even the digression on Typhaon, awkwardly inserted as it is, fits well into the themes of the poem and may well be part of the reshaped poem rather than a later interpolation. A scholiast at Pindar's *Nemean* 2.1 claimed that one of

[24] *The Iliad of Homer, Translated by Mr. Pope* (1715), I, sig. F2.

[25] Chapman frequently follows his own sense of the structure of a scene, choosing to indent a line which Spondanus's Greek text does not, but at 178 (Chapman 278) neither Spondanus nor Chapman saw reason to indicate a shift in the narrative.

the Homeridai, a poet named Cynaethus of Chios, composed verses in Homer's name, including the *Hymn to Apollo*, and was the first to recite Homer's poems at Syracuse, in the 69th Olympiad (=504/501 BCE). The date seems too late for the original compositions of either part of the *Hymn to Apollo* but, if there is truth to the observation, it may be the case that Cynaethus was the one to reshape two older poems into the poem found in this collection. If so, this would be the only poem in this grouping with an identifiable author.

The *Hymn to Hermes* (Mercury) (#4) (580 lines in Greek; 1011 in Chapman). This is the longest of the *Hymns*, and certainly the last of the long hymns to be composed. It is also among the wittiest and most playful in keeping with the trickster nature of the god it celebrates. Born of Zeus and Maia, a goddess from the line of crafty Prometheus and Iapetus, the "faire tongu'd, but false hearted" (Chapman, *A Hymne to Hermes* 20), Hermes might easily have grown up to threaten the new order of Olympus so celebrated in Hesiod's *Theogony*. As much as he exasperates his older brother Apollo when, not even a day old, he steals the far-shooter's prized cattle, the irrepressible newcomer is eager to be accepted by his father and welcomed into the company of the Olympians. He gains this end by his characteristic craft and whimsy: less than six hours old, he invents the lyre by slaying a tortoise and fitting a bridge and seven strings to the back of the hollowed-out shell. Trying his hand at this "lovely plaything," he improvised a song—about his parent's love affair and his own distinguished lineage, naturally enough. In the early hours of his second day, by the river Alpheios he invents a device for making fire, wrestles two of Apollo's mighty cattle to the ground and slays them, roasting their meat (careful not to eat any of it himself). Without explanation, Hermes has divided the meat into twelve portions with a "perfect honor for each" (4.129). It is generally presumed that Hermes is preparing a sacrifice for the twelve Olympian gods, *implicitly* including himself in that number and reversing Prometheus's unequal division of sacrificial meats at Mecone that greatly angered Zeus, as described in Hesiod's *Theogony* (536–49). In Zeus's presence, the two brothers eventually reconcile, when Hermes returns the surviving cattle and gives to his older brother the plaything that he had invented the day before. Created on a whim, the lyre will become an integral part of Apollo's identity and acquire the greatest significance for gods (and men), the instrument associated with the highest art, festivity, song and dance, and Olympian harmony. Needless to say, by hymn's end Hermes has gained acceptance on Mt. Olympus. Like Apollo in the *Hymn to Apollo*, the potentially dangerous Hermes in this hymn proves from the start to be a loyal, if irreverent, member of his father's new order.

The tone and clever arrangement of episodes in the hymn elegantly imitates Hermes' character. As do the other long hymns, this one appears to allude to the establishment of the cult, in this case that of the Twelve Gods at Olympia (along the Alpheios), and it could well be that the hymn was composed for festivities there. Though the origin of this cult is much older, diction and untraditional use of formulae suggest a fifth-century date for the hymn. Narrative inconsistencies and repetitions make translation difficult but Chapman often captures the humor and light touch of the poem.

The *Hymn to Aphrodite* (Venus) (#5) (293 lines in Greek; 487 in Chapman). This is the shortest of the long hymns and most likely the oldest. It is closely associated with Troy and has close parallels with the *Iliad*, causing some scholars to argue that it might have been by Homer. It probably dates to the end of the seventh century. As in Homer, but contrary to the story of her birth in Hesiod's *Theogony*, in this hymn Aphrodite is identified as Zeus's daughter. She is also called the Cyprian goddess, and Kytherea, after the two islands associated with her sea-birth in the *Theogony* (188–200). These names for the goddess need not evoke Hesiod's tale, however, as Aphrodite's association with Cyprus and her cult center at Paphos appears to date back to the twelfth century, long before either poet.

Again, the hymn treats playfully a theme important to Hesiod's *Theogony*. Rather than transforming the generative but destabilizing force of eros as he does in Hesiod's poem, in the hymn Zeus turns the tables on Aphrodite, subjecting her to the bewitching powers of love that have bedeviled him and most other gods. Driven by Zeus to fall in love with a mortal, Aphrodite seduces the Trojan prince Anchises on Mt. Ida. Shamed by her pregnancy, she insists that the child be named Aeneas (Aineias) "because a dreadful / distress (*ainos / akhos*) took hold of me, that I fell into the bed of a mortal man" (198–99). Chapman movingly embellishes these verses, with the end rhyme of "life" and "griefe," and the added line in the second couplet (327–30), but he misses the pun on Aineias and *ainos* in the Greek (as does Dartona's Latin translation: Huic autem et Aeneas nomen erit. Quoniam me gravis / Habuit dolor, quod mortalis viri incidi ad lectum):

> His Name Aeneas—therein keeping life
> For ever in my much-conceipted griefe,
> That I (immortall) fell into the bed
> Of one whose blood Mortality must shed.

A comparison of three love unions at the end allows meditation on sexual energy and renewal. Eos (Dawn) at the edge of the world offers her mortal lover immortality but not eternal youth in what proves to be a sterile union. Zeus whisks his beloved, Ganymedes, the adolescent son of Laomedon, up to Olympus to join the gods in what is also—this time of necessity—a union without procreation. Aphrodite, by contrast, beds down in love with the mortal Anchises on the wild slopes of Mt. Ida. The union in the realm of men is fertile, leading to a kind of urban immortality—Aeneas will die but give birth to an unending line of rulers at Troy (197).

The *Hymn to Aphrodite* (To the Same) (#6) (21 lines in Greek; 32 in Chapman). This hymn charmingly embellishes Hesiod's account of Aphrodite's birth from the sea as told in the *Theogony* (188–200), though there is no mention of her birth from Heaven's genitals. In this hymn, the Horae (Seasons) attend Aphrodite as she comes ashore. Angelo Poliziano, a scholar and poet whom Chapman admired, draws from this hymn in his *Stanze Cominciate per la Giostra del Magnifico Giuliano de' Medici* I.99–101 (1478), and it is Poliziano's poem which influenced Botticelli's *Birth of Venus* (c. 1485). Spenser also draws from this hymn in *The Faerie Queene* 4.12.2 (1596). The last lines of the hymn explicitly refer to rhapsodic performance, perhaps at Aphrodite's ancient sanctuary at Paphos, though nothing in the hymn indicates the date of composition.

The *Hymn to Dionysus* (#7) (Bacchus or The Pyrats) (#7) (59 lines in Greek; 103 in Chapman). This hymn is our earliest source for the famous story of pirates attempting to abduct Dionysus. Dates from the seventh to fifth century have been suggested for the hymn, most likely placing it before a black-figure cup by Exekias (circa 530 BCE) depicting Dionysus reclining on board a ship with a grape vine sprouting above the mast and dolphins dancing around the vessel. Because of the hymn, some imagine that the dolphins, a commonplace image for the sea on vases, stand in for the pirates. In the sixth century, in ritual the arrival of the god featured men carrying a seated Dionysus in an ivy-wreathed ship with his priest as helmsman. Nothing in the poem reveals a probable place of composition.

The *Hymn to Ares* (Mars) (#8) (17 lines in Greek, 36 in Chapman). This hymn is probably by the Neoplatonist Proclus (fifth century CE) and found its way into this collection by accident. The hymn does not follow the typical formulaic structure of the others; furthermore, its string of epithets is characteristic of late hymns, as is the double focus on anthropomorphic and planetary aspects of the god. The poet's prayer to Ares is also anomalous.

The *Hymn to Artemis* (Diana) (#9) (8 lines in Greek; 15 in Chapman). Nothing in the hymn suggests the date of composition, though Smyrna was destroyed around 600 BCE. The hymn was probably performed there or for a festival at Apollo/Artemis/Leto's cult center at Klaros near Smyrna.

The *Hymn to Aphrodite* (Venus) (#10) (6 lines in Greek; 12 in Chapman). Like #6, this hymn stresses Aphrodite's presence on Cyprus; the prominence of Cypriote Salamis (cf. 5.292) in the hymn may indicate that it was performed there. There is no evidence for dating. In the echo of *himertos / himeroeis* (*amabilis* in Dartona's Latin translation), the hymn draws attention to the similarity between Aphrodite's allure or loveliness and that of song. Chapman renders two of the three appearances of the word with "desire."

The *Hymn to Athena* (Pallas) (#11) (5 lines in Greek; 10 in Chapman). There is no evidence within the hymn to suggest date or locale of composition. As a god's power is realized both in a positive and in a negative form, here Athena is both "Patronesse of Cities" and sacker of cities, a role she performs with Ares, though Chapman stresses that "at both times Shee / All injur'de people sets on foot and free."

The *Hymn to Hera* (Juno) (#12) (5 lines in Greek; 8 in Chapman). This hymn stresses Hera's regality, suggested in her epithet golden-throned, and her revered status, quite unlike Zeus's humiliating treatment of her in the *Iliad* or her rage at Zeus in the *Theogony* and the *Hymn to Apollo* #3 for usurping the female power to give birth. Nothing in the hymn suggests a date or place of performance.

The *Hymn to Demeter* (Ceres) (#13) (3 lines in Greek; 8 in Chapman). Though it is the shortest of the hymns, it still shows hymnic features at both opening and close. It also emphasizes the bond between mother and daughter. It is not possible to determine the date or place of composition.

The *Hymn to the Mother of the Gods* (#14) (6 lines in Greek; 10 in Chapman). This hymn refers to the ancient Anatolian Mother Goddess, who by the seventh century BCE is known as Cybele, though in this hymn she is not named. The date and place of composition are uncertain.

The *Hymn to Heracles the Lion-Hearted* (Hercules) (#15) (9 lines in Greek; 16 in Chapman). This hymn stresses the eventual immortality of one born from a mortal woman and a god, a process of deification that Heracles first experiences formally in the sixth century in Attica. The hymn may therefore be from that time and locale. The epithet "lion-hearted" (*leontothumos*) is elsewhere unattested in Greek.

The *Hymn to Asclepius* (Aesculapius) *(#16)* (5 lines in Greek; 8 in Chapman). Asclepius, the son of Apollo and a mortal woman named Coronis, is a physician and here a "worthy King." According to Pindar, he was killed by Zeus for bringing a mortal back to life; in the Hellenistic period at Epidauros and Kos, he was worshipped as a god. This hymn offers no hint of the standard story that Coronis was killed by Apollo (or Artemis) for sleeping with a man, the baby being rescued by Apollo from his mother's womb and entrusted to the Centaur, Chiron, who taught him the art of healing. It is difficult to determine the time or place of composition.

The *Hymn to the Dioscuri* (Castor and Pollux) (#17) (5 lines in Greek; 10 in Chapman). This hymn seems to be an abbreviated version of #33.

The *Hymn to Hermes* (Mercurie) (#18) (12 lines in Greek; 18 in Chapman). In the Greek, 18.2–10 is almost identical to 4.2–10 though one would never know that from Chapman's different translations of these two passages. The first ten lines of Hymn 18 comprise one sentence in the Greek text, a feat Chapman imitated in 18.1–14.

The *Hymn to Pan* (#19) (49 lines in Greek; 84 in Chapman). Pan, son of Hermes, is an Arcadian god, who is also worshipped in Athens after the Battle of Marathon (490 BCE). His popularity grew throughout Greece in the fifth century. This is one of the latest hymns, dating most likely from 500–450 BCE and of unknown provenience. Lines 28–34 appear to be influenced by the fifth-century *Hymn to Hermes* (#4), lines 2–4.

The *Hymn to Hephaestus* (Vulcan) (#20) (8 lines in Greek; 12 in Chapman). As happens in this hymn, Athens linked Athena and Hephaestus: "Who, with the skie-eyd Pallas, first did give / Men rules of buildings, that before did live / In Caves and Denns and Hills like savage Beasts"; the city even honored them in a shared cult. The idea of human evolution from a primitive state was made popular by the sophist Protagoras in the fifth century. It is possible that the hymn is from Athens toward the end of that century.

The *Hymn to Apollo* (Phoebus) (#21) (5 lines in Greek; 8 in Chapman). The Peneus referred to in line 3 was a river in Thessaly. Callimachus in the *Hymn to Apollo* (line 7) and in the *Hymn to Delos* (lines 375–85) also associates Apollo with the swan, though this evidence need not indicate either place or time of composition.

The *Hymn to Poseidon* (Neptune) (#22) (7 lines in Greek; 10 in Chapman). There is no record of Poseidon being worshipped at (Mt.) Helicon in Boeotia. The cities Helice and Aegae near Corinth were sacred to Poseidon (*Iliad* 8.203) and he was worshipped as *Helikônios* among the Ionian cities on the Asia Minor coast. It is tempting to think that there is some confusion about place names in the hymn. Both the time and place of composition remain uncertain.

The *Hymn to Zeus* (Jove) (#23) (4 lines in Greek; 10 in Chapman). Zeus's sexual union with Themis (Law, Custom) is especially significant in the *Theogony* 901–6. Their children, the three Horae—Eunomia (Good Governance), Dike (Justice), and Eirene (Social Peace)—allow Olympus and the human polis to keep Eris's (Discord's) children—Dusnomia, Pseudea (Lies), and Neikea (Quarrels)—at bay. The low profile of Zeus in the hymn collection and the number of allusions to—or parallels with—the *Theogony* suggest that the collection as a whole was thought to complement Hesiod's creation poem.

The *Hymn to Hestia* (Vesta) (#24) (5 lines in Greek; 9 in Chapman). Hestia is often referred to as the first- and last-born from Cronus, as she was the first to be conceived (and swallowed) and therefore the last to be regurgitated from Cronus's stomach. She is thus Zeus's oldest and youngest sister, a virgin goddess and guardian of both the urban and domestic hearth. Though she is associated with Apollo at Delphi in this hymn, the invocation to Zeus may refer to a location other than Delphi and the house may be a temple of the two gods rather than a private home. It is difficult to determine either the time or place of the hymn's composition.

The *Hymn to the Muses and Apollo* (#25) (7 lines in Greek, 8 in Chapman). This hymn paraphrases *Theogony* 1, 94–7, 104.

The *Hymn to Dionysus* (Bacchus) (#26) (13 lines in Greek; 22 in Chapman). This hymn refers obliquely to Dionysus's birth from Zeus's thigh. The last lines show that it was performed annually at a festival, though it is impossible to determine where and when it was composed.

The *Hymn to Artemis* (Diana) (#27) (22 lines in Greek; 36 in Chapman). This hymn shows similarities with the long hymn to her brother, *Hymn to Apollo* (#3), and probably dates from the same time.

The *Hymn to Athena* (Pallas) (#28) (18 lines in Greek; 26 in Chapman). The hymn's celebration of the birth of Athena (which so enraged Hera) is also celebrated in the *Theogony* 886–90 and 924–26 and in sixth-century vase paintings as well as in sixth-century choral lyric poets like Stesichorus. Hesiod does not mention that she was born in full armor, though this is a common feature in sixth-century poetry and art. As with Hymn #27, the style of this hymn has much in common with the *Hymn to Apollo* (#3).

The *Hymn to Hestia* (Vesta and Mercurie) (#29) (14 lines in Greek; 30 in Chapman). Both gods were associated with the protection of the home and it is possible that this may be a private hymn. We do not hear elsewhere that Hestia was the first to receive libations, though her prominence as a hearth goddess would make this practice likely. Elsewhere, Hermes also appears to be honored with the last libation (cf. *Odyssey* 7.137–38). Nothing in the hymn indicates either the place or time of composition.

The *Hymn to Earth, Mother of All* (#30) (19 lines in Greek; 33 in Chapman). This hymn describes Earth's natural bounty, though unlike many of the other poems in the collection, this one is free of personification (parents, sexual partners, children). It thus is probably of late composition.

*Hymns to Helios* (Sun) (#31) (19 lines in Greek; 36 in Chapman) and *to Selene* (Moon) (#32) (20 lines in Greek; 28 in Chapman). Neither deity was important in cult. Stylistic analysis suggests single authorship and late composition for both hymns.

The *Hymn to the Dioscuri* (Castor and Pollux) (#33) (19 lines in Greek; 26 in Chapman). Frequently in myth, these twins are regarded as mortal. In other versions, Castor is mortal, fathered by Tyndareus, while Poulydeuces is immortal, sired by Zeus on the same night as Tyndareus fathered Castor. When Castor is killed, his brother forsakes his immortality so that the twins may spend half their time together in the underworld and half on Olympus. In local Spartan cult both may have been elevated to divine status. Scholars see parallels with the *Hymn to Dionysus* (#7), another "mortal god." Nothing is said in the hymn of their sisters, Clytaemnestra, daughter of Tyndareus, and Helen, sired by Zeus in swan form. The twins' association with stormy seas and rescuing sailors is traditional but odd as Sparta is an inland city. A sixth-century inscription from the island of Kephallenia, north and west of Sparta, combines a phrase from line 9 of the hymn and *Iliad* 2.631, perhaps suggesting an early date for this hymn.

Poem to *Xenoi* (Men of Hospitalitie) (5 lines in Greek; 8 in Chapman). How this poem (not a hymn) got into this collection is not clear. It is not found in all of the manuscripts.

*Batrachomyomachia* (303 lines in Greek; 444 in Chapman). The
hostilities between frogs and mice begins innocently enough
when the king of the frogs, Cheekpuffer or Puffjawe (Physigna-
thos) kindly offers to convey Crumbsnatcher or Filchcrumble
(Psicharpax) on his back across a lake. Events turn sore when
the frog, threatened by a water snake, dives deep into the water,
causing the poor mouse to expire in the water. Parodying epic
scenes and formulae, it offers an amusing spoof on Homer and
was attributed to him by some in antiquity; others assign com-
position to a Carian by the name of Pigres. In Spondanus's
*Homeri Quae Extant Omnia* and in Chapman's *The Crowne of all
Homers Workes,* the mock epic comes after the *Odyssey* and be-
fore the *Hymns.* In modern times, it is rarely read and, if pub-
lished at all, it comes after the *Hymns,* as for example in West's
Loeb edition that includes both the hymns and Homeric apoc-
rypha. It is first mentioned in the first century CE and is prob-
ably of that era. The tradition of animal stories, as in Aesop's
Fables and this epic narrative, is certainly as old as Homer's
heroic epic. Much of the humor consists in burlesque epi-
thets and ponderous preposterous polysyllabic proper names.
Chapman, like Aldus Manutius in his Latin gloss accompany-
ing Spondanus's Greek text, merely transliterates the Greek
names, failing thus to capture much of the humor in the mock
epic but, especially with alliteration, he makes a noble stab at
rendering the poem's light tone; for example, "Limnocharis,
beholding Polyphon / Thus done to death, did, with as round
a stone . . . " (306–7). While Coleridge was wrong about the
date of composition, his assessment conforms with the view of
many today: "I am so dull, that neither in the original nor in
any translation could I ever find any wit or wise purpose in
this poem. The whole humor seems to lie in the names. The
frogs and mice are not frogs or mice, but men, and yet they do
nothing that conveys any satire. In the Greek there is much

beauty of language, but the joke is very flat. This is always the case in rude ages;—their serious vein is inimitable,—their comic low, and low indeed. The psychological cause is easily stated, and copiously exemplifiable."[26] Homer and Pigres were also credited with composing the satiric *Margites* (*margo*s = impetuous), a poem (mostly lost except for a few lines found on papyri) about a simpleton, born of rich parents, who among other travails needs to be coaxed with ludicrous difficulty on his wedding night to perform his marital duties.

The Epigrams are culled from the pseudo-Herodotean *Life of Homer* and other late documents such as the *Contest of Homer and Hesiod*, a text which in its present form dates to the Antonine period (second century CE) but derives from a fourth-century BCE Athenian source, if not from an earlier one. Unlike Homer's *Iliad* and *Odyssey*, many of these short poems are in the first-person singular and offer facts about Homer's life that some in antiquity took as gospel but to which the Alexandrian librarians paid little heed. Other epigrams offer words of wisdom or give voice to a place, a tombstone, a tree, or a person from Homer's epic poems. Compared to his rousing Iliadic fourteeners and his more delicate pentameter couplets of the *Odysses* and *Hymni*, Chapman's pentameters in his translations of the epigrams show him struggling. But, having completed them, he is free to write:[27]

> The Worke that I was borne to doe is done.
> Glory to Him that the Conclusion
> Makes the beginning of my life; and Never
> Let me be said to live, till I live Ever.

[26] Whalley, ed., *The Collected Works of Samuel Taylor Coleridge*, vol. 12:II, p. 1126.
[27] Chapman's epigram at the end of *The Crowne of all Homers Workes*, lines 2–4.

# EDITOR'S INTRODUCTION

In CHAPMAN's *Iliads* breathes a vigorous, impetuous spirit, the excitement of a poet who sees in Achilles a prime representative of the manly virtues. The atmosphere of the *Odysses* is more placid, in keeping with the translator's double discovery that not all which had seemed virtuous in Achilles was indeed so and that a nobler soul might be found in the sorely-tried Ulysses, the man made wise through suffering. Even although he has infused into both these works much of his own changing philosophy and has departed from or added to his original, Chapman deserves Keats' praise for both. Here is the realm of gold expressed in Elizabethan terms.

Perhaps not so much may be said for the *Batrachomyomachia*, the *Hymns* and the *Epigrams*. The noticeable decline in poetic inspiration manifest in these poems seems to be due to several things. First, we get the impression that in essaying the translation of the lesser poems, Chapman was not truly impelled to his task, but was intent merely on 'finishing off' his Homer. Secondly, it is obvious that he could find here no opportunity for interpreting the original Greek in his own characteristic way; there was no hero with whom he could identify himself. Thirdly, we feel that, despite his philosophical tendencies, Chapman's genius found finest scope in the narrative and dramatic kinds, particularly when the subject-matter permitted a rich flow of noble rhetoric. His hand was too heavy to deal successfully with the light burlesque of the battle of the frogs and mice, and in the *Hymns* and *Epigrams* he was given but little opportunity for the telling of a story. A fourth element of weakness is to be traced in his actual understanding of the Greek original. He had made some mistakes in the *Iliads* and the *Odysses*, but most of his deviations from the original were deliberate. Again and again we get the impression not so much of a man uncertain concerning the true meaning of the Greek, but sure in his own soul that by inspiration he has divined a sense which has passed the scholars by. In the later poems only too often we watch Chapman utterly mistaking the original sense or so baffled that he can wrest no sense whatsoever from the Greek lines. Finally, it must be admitted that the stylistic crabbedness which is to be discerned in all his writings increased as the years went by, and even when he knew clearly what he wanted to say he now found his means of expression inadequate to convey his thoughts. Favourite words and expressions are now tortured almost beyond belief, and sometimes the simplest thoughts are forced to assume circumlocutionary forms which at first reading, sometimes even at later readings, seem meaningless.

Perhaps the most interesting aspect of this work is the way in which it demonstrates Chapman's self-identification with Homer. The dedicatory verses addressed to the Earl of Somerset and the final lines in which he provides a valedictory to his self-assumed task indicate this most clearly, but repeatedly in the translations the same note is struck. Accepting the universal view that the *Hymns* and the *Epigrams* were genuinely the work of Homer, he seizes every opportunity of identifying his fate with the presumed lot of the Greek poet—a man of supreme greatness whose words had not been given their due meed of praise, who had been neglected by the rabble and who had moved through life poverty-stricken and esteemed only by an intellectual few. The manner in which Chapman's verses strike sudden fire whenever he comes to a passage which permits him to express contempt and detestation of his detractors tells its own story.

Precisely when *The Crowne of all Homers Workes* appeared or was written is difficult to determine, but certainly several years must have elapsed after the *Odysses* of 1614 before it was completed. Perhaps 1624 is as near a guess as we can make to its date of publication. Although he was a chronic grumbler, in one thing Chapman must always have considered himself fortunate. His *Iliads* and *Odysses* are handsome volumes, and for his *Crowne* he found an important printer-bookseller willing to produce an equally handsome folio, on the whole carefully printed and amply—indeed, perhaps over-amply—spaced. The volume has an elaborate engraved title page which must have pleased the author greatly, for it shows a laurel-crowned Homer, heavy-bearded, and, directly below, a portrait of an equally heavily bearded Chapman, the latter even more prominent than the former. Homer is backed by a trio of deities—Apollo holding a musical instrument, Hermes with his caduceus, and a buxom Pallas. The lower frame of the title page, besides Chapman's portrait, with the motto *"Conscium evasi diem,"* surrounded by clouds, has illustrations of the battle of the frogs and the mice, eagles flying above, and the title itself:

the

CROWNE of all HOMERS WORKES
Batrachomyomachia

*Or the Battaile of Frogs and Mise.*
His Hymn's ——— and ——— Epigrams

*Translated according to y<sup>e</sup> Originall*
By George Chapman.

At the foot is the bookseller's announcement: London, *Printed by* Iohn Bill, *his* MAIESTIES *Printer.* *"Pass: fecit"* appears at the bottom of the frame to the right, indicating that this engraving was the work of William Pass (Willem van de Passe).

The volume itself, apart from the title page, consists of 100 leaves, with signatures ¶⁴, A—Z⁴, Aa². For the dedicatory verses a roman font is used; the rest, except for the Latin prayer at the end and for proper names, is in large italic. In some copies "WORKES" appears as "WORCKES."

The Widener Library at Harvard University possesses a copy which has a manuscript dedication in Chapman's own hand:

> In loue and honor of yᵉ Righte Virtuouse and
> worthie Gent: Mʳ Henry Reynolds,
> And to crowne all his deseruings
> wᵗʰ eternall Memorie
> Geo: Chapman
> Joines this Crowne and Conclusion
> of all the Homericall Meritts wᵗʰ his
> Accomplisht Improuements;
> Aduising
> That if at first sighte he seme darck
> Or too fierie He will yet holde
> him fast (like Proteus)
> Till he appere in his propper similitude
> And he will then shewe him
> self—Vatem egregiu cui non sit publics Vena
> Qui Nihil expositum soleat deducere; nec qui
> Communi feriat Carmen triuiale moneta.

Two corrections of the text in Chapman's hand have been incorporated in the present edition.

In general, the same principles have been employed here as were applied for the texts of the *Iliads* and the *Odysses*, except that the introductory verses have been printed in italic and

the italic text in roman. The punctuation of the original has
been entirely abandoned, since it is hopelessly erratic and in
numerous passages rather puzzling. Two examples will serve.
The first is *A Hymne to Hermes,* II. 98–104:

> *His word,*
> *And worke, had individuall accord.*
> *All being as swiftly to perfection brought;*
> *As any worldly mans, most rauisht thought,*
> *Whose minde, Care cuts, in an infinity*
> *Of varied parts, or passions instantly;*
> *Or as the frequent twincklings of an eye.*

The same hymn, II. 379–82, provides another example:

> *But last Evening late,*
> *I sawe a Thing, that shew'd of childish state;*
> *To my ould lights; and seem'd as he pursude*
> *A Herd of Oxen.*

Instead of an attempt to modify the original, it seemed better
boldly to repunctuate the entire text.

As in the second part of the *Odysses,* a few possessive nouns
have apostrophes in the original, and, for the sake of com-
pleteness of record, these are noted here: *An Hymne to Apollo,*
I. 52. "Ida's", I. 154 "Saturnia's," I. 609 "Delphusa's," I. 834
"Latona's"; *A Hymne to Hermes,* I. 142 "Pieria's," I. 192 "Phoe-
bus-Apollo's," I. 299 "Latona's," I. 300 "Apollo's," I. 333 "La-
tona's," I. 353 "Latona's," I. 419 "Maia's," I. 426 "Apollo's," I.
463 "Latona's," I. 504 "Apollo's," I. 899 "Mercurie's," II. 911,
967, 992 and 1001 "Maia's"; *To Mars,* I. 9 *"Fortitud's"*; *To
Castor and Pollux,* I. 4 "Leda's"; *To Mercurie,* I. 11 "Iuno's," I.
15 "Maia's"; *To Diana,* I. 35 "Latona's"; *To Pallas,* I. 1 "Pallas-
Minerua's"; *To Men of Hospitalitie,* I. 5 "Pluto's"; *Cuma refusing*

*his Offer,* I. 28 "Cuma's". All the other possessive apostrophes in the present text have been inserted.

No attempt has been made to follow the typographical setting out of the titles and end-lines of the separate poems. Rather irregularly the words 'he' and 'all' are printed in Chapman's text as 'He' and 'All': for the most part the capitals have been retained, but in a few instances, where confusion might arise, the capitals have been reduced to lower case and have been so marked in the notes.

A number of brackets indicating triple rhymes, omitted in the original text, have been added; and in one instance such a bracket in the original has been omitted because, in fact, four rhymes, not three, are concerned.

*—Allardyce Nicoll*

*The Crowne of all Homers Workes*

# TO
## MY EVER
## MOST-WORTHIE-TO-BE-MOST-HONOR'D LORD
### THE EARLE OF SOMERSET, &c

Not forc't by fortune, but since your free minde  )  
(Made by affliction) rests in choice resign'd      }  
To calme Retreate, laid quite beneath the winde  )  
Of Grace and Glory, I well know, my Lord,  
You would not be entitl'd to a word                          5  
That might a thought remove from your Repose  )  
To thunder and spit Flames, as Greatnesse does,  }  
For all the Trumps that still tell where he goes.  )  
Of which Trumps Dedication being One,  
Me thinks I see you start to heare it blowne.                10  
But this is no such Trump as summons Lords  
Gainst Envie's steele to draw their leaden swords,  
Or gainst Hare-lipt Detraction, Contempt,  
All which from all Resistance stand exempt,  
It being as hard to sever Wrong from Merit                   15  
As meate-indude from blood, or blood from spirit.  
Nor in the spirit's Chariot rides the soule  
In bodies chaste with more divine controule,  
Nor virtue shines more in a lovely Face,  
Than true desert is stuck off with Disgrace.                 20  
And therefore truth it selfe, that had to blesse  
The merit of it all, Almightinesse,  
Would not protect it from the Bane and Ban  
Of all Moodes most distraught and Stygian—  
As counting it the Crowne of all Desert,                     25  
Borne to Heaven, to take of Earth no part  
Of false Joy here, for Joyes-there-endlesse troth,  
Nor sell his Birthright for a messe of Broth,

But stay and still sustaine, and his Blisse bring,
Like to the hatching of the Black-thorne's spring,          30
With bitter frosts and smarting haile-stormes, forth.
Fates love Bees' labors; onely Paine crownes Worth.
This Dedication calls no Greatnes then
To patrone this Greatnes-creating Penn,
Nor you to add to your dead calme a breath;                 35
For those arm'd Angells, that in spight of death
Inspir'd those flowrs that wrought this poet's wreath,
Shall keepe it ever Poesie's steepest Starr,
As, in Earth's flaming wals, Heaven's sevenfold Carr
(From all the wildes of Neptune's watrie sphere)           40
For ever guards the Erymanthian Beare.

    Since then your Lordship settles in your shade
A life retir'd, and no Retreate is made
But to some strength (for else tis no Retreate,
But rudely running from your Battaile's heate),            45
I give this as your strength: your strength, my Lord,
In Counsailes and Examples, that, afford
More Guard than whole Hosts of corporeal powre,
And more deliverance teach the fatall Howre.

    Turne not your medcine then to your disease,       50
By your too set and sleight repulse of these,
The Adjuncts of your matchlesse Odysses;
Since on that wisest minde of Man relies
Refuge from all Live's Infelicities.

    Nor sing these such division from them,             55
But that these spinn the thred of the same streame
From one selfe Distaff's stuff: for Poesie's Pen
(Through al theames) is t'informe the lives of Men,
All whose Retreates neede strengths of all degrees—
Without which (had you even Herculean knees)               60
Your foes' fresh Charges would at length prevaile,

# To the Earle of Somerset

*To leave your Noblest suff'rance no least saile.*
*Strength then the Object is of all Retreates;*
*Strength needes no friend's trust, strength your foes defeates.*
*Retire to strength, then, of eternall things,*                          65
*And y'are eternall; for our knowing Springs*
*Flow into those things that we truely know,*
*Which (being Eternall) we are render'd so.*
*And though your high-fixt Light passe infinite farr*
*Th'advicefull Guide of my still-trembling Starr,*                       70
*Yet heare what my dischardg'd Peece must foretell,*
*Standing, your Poore and Perdue Sentinell.*
*Kings may perhaps wish even your Beggar's Voice*
*To their Eternities, how skorn'd a choice*
*Soever now it lies; And (dead) I may*                                   75
*Extend your life to light's extreamest Raie.*
*If not, your Homer yet past doubt shall make*
*Immortall, like himselfe, your Bountie's stake*
*Put in my hands, to propagate your Fame;*
*Such virtue reigns in such united Name.*                                80
  *Retire to him then for advice and skill.*[1]    ⎫
*To know things call'd worst Best, and Best most ill.*  ⎬
*Which knowne, truths best chuse, and retire to still.*  ⎭
*And as our English Generall (whose Name*
*Shall equall interest finde in th'House of Fame*                        85
*With all Earth's great'st Commanders), in Retreate*
*To Belgian Gant, stood all Spaine's Armies' heate*
*By Parma led, though but one thousand strong;*
*Three miles together thrusting through the throng*
*Of th'Enimies' Horse (still pouring on their Fall*                      90
*Twixt him and home) and thunderd through them al;*
*The Gallick Monsiour standing on the wall,*

---

[1] A simile illustrating the most renownd service of Generall Noris in his Retreate before Cant, never before made sacred to Memorie.

*And wondring at his dreadfull Discipline,*
*Fir'd with a Valor that spit spirit Divine;*
*In five Battaillons randging all his Men,*         95
*Bristl'd with Pikes, and flanck't with Flanckers ten;*
*Gave fire still in his Rere; retir'd and wrought*
*Downe to his fixt strength still, retir'd and fought;*
*All the Battaillons of the Enemie's Horse*
*Storming upon him still their fieriest Force;*        100
*Charge upon Charge laid fresh; he, fresh as day,*
*Repulsing all, and forcing glorious way*
*Into the Gates, that gaspt (as swounes, for Ayre)*
*And looke their life in with untoucht Repaire:*
*So fight out, sweet Earle, your Retreate in Peace;*        105
*No ope-warr equalls that where privie Prease*
*Of never-numberd odds of Enimie,*   ⎫
*Arm'd all by Envie, in blinde Ambush lie,*   ⎬
*To rush out like an open threatning skie,*   ⎭
*Broke al in Meteors round about your eares.*        110
*Gainst which (though far from hence) through al your Reres*
*Have fires prepar'd; wisdome with wisdome flanck,*
*And all your forces randge in present ranck;*
*Retiring as you now fought in your strength,*
*From all the Force laid, in time's utmost length,*        115
*To charge, and basely come on you behind.*   ⎫
*The Doctrine of all which you here shall finde,*   ⎬
*And in the true Glasse of a humane Minde—*   ⎭
*Your Odysses—the Body letting see*
*All his life past, through Infelicitie,*        120
*And manage of it all. In which to friend,*
*The full Muse brings you both the prime and end*
*Of all Arts ambient in the Orbe of Man;*
*Which never darknesse most Cimmerian*
*Can give Eclipse, since (blinde) He all things sawe,*        125

# To the Earle of Somerset

*And to all, ever since, liv'd Lord and Lawe.*
*And though our mere-learn'd men, and Modern wise,* ⎫
*Taste not poore Poesie's Ingenuities,* ⎬
*Being crusted with their covetous Leprosies,* ⎭
*But hold her paines worse than the spider's worke,*                    130
*And lighter than the shadowe of a Corke,*
*Yet th'ancient learn'd, heat with celestiall fire,*
*Affirmes her flames so sacred and entire*
*That not without God's greatest grace she can*
*Fall in the wid'st Capacitie of Man.*[2]                    135
   *If yet the vile Soule of this Verminous time* ⎫
*Love more the Sale-Muse, and the Squirrel's chime,* ⎬
*Than this full sphere of Poesie's sweetest Prime,* ⎭
*Give them unenvied their vaine veine and vent,*
*And rest your wings in his approv'd Ascent*                    140
*That yet was never reacht, nor ever fell*
*Into affections bought with things that sell,*
*Being the Sunn's Flowre, and wrapt so in his skie*
*He cannot yeeld to every Candle's eye.*

> Whose most worthy Discoveries to your
> Lordship's Judiciall Perspective in most
> subdude Humilitie submitteth,
>          —*GEORGE CHAPMAN*

[2] Ut non sine Maximo favore Dei comparari queat. Pla. in Ione.

# To the Earle of Somerset

## The Occasion of this Impos'd
### CROWNE

    After this not onely Prime of Poets, but Philosophers,
had written his two great Poems of Iliads and Odysses
—which (for their first Lights borne before all Learn-
ing) were worthily call'd the Sunne and Moone of the
Earth—(finding no compensation) he writ in contempt     5
of Men this ridiculous Poem of Vermin, giving them
Nobility of Birth, valorous elocution not inferior to his
Heroes At which the Gods themselves, put in amaze,
call'd Counsailes about their assistance of either Armie,
and the justice of their Quarrels, even to the mount-     10
ing of Jove's Artillery against them, and discharge of
his three-forckt flashes: and all for the drowning of a
Mouse. After which sleight and onely recreative touch,
hee betooke him seriously to the honor of the Gods, in
Hymns resounding all their peculiar Titles, Jurisdic-     15
tion, and Dignities; which hee illustrates at all parts as
he had been continually conversant amongst them: and
whatsoever autentique Poesie he omitted in the Episods
contained in his Iliads and Odysses, he comprehends
and concludes in his Hymns and Epigrams. Al his     20
observance and honor of the Gods rather mov'd their
envies against him than their rewards, or respects of his
endevours. And so like a Man *verecundi ingenii* (which
he witnesseth of himselfe) he liv'd unhonord and needie
till his death; yet notwithstanding all men's servile     25
and manacled Miseries to his most absolute and never-
equall'd Merite—yea even bursten profusion to Impos-
ture and Impiety—heare our ever-the-Same intranced
and never-sleeping Master of the Muses, to his last
accent incomparablie singing.     30

AL THE HYMNES OF HOMER

# AN HYMNE TO APOLLO

I will remember and expresse the praise
Of heaven's far-darter, the faire King of daies,
Whom even the Gods themselves feare when he goes
Through Jove's high house; and when his goodly bowes
He goes to bend, all from their Thrones arise,                5
And cluster neare t'admire his faculties.
Onely Latona stirs not from her seate
Close by the Thunderer, till her sonne's retreat
From his dread archerie; but then she goes,
Slackens his string, and shuts his Quiver close,             10
And (having taken to her hand his bowe
From off his able shoulders) doth bestowe
Upon a Pinne of gold the glorious Tiller,
The Pinne of gold fixt in his Father's Piller.
    Then doth she to his Throne his state uphold,            15
Where his great Father in a cup of gold
Serves him with Nectar, and shews all the grace
Of his great sonne. Then th'other gods take place,
His gracious mother glorying to beare
So great an Archer and a sonne so cleare.                    20
    All haile (O blest Latona!) to bring forth
An issue of such All-out-shining worth,
Royall Apollo, and the Queene that loves
The hurles of darts. She in th'Ortygian groves,
And he in cliffie Delos, leaning on                          25
The loftie Oros, and being built upon
By Cynthus' Prominent, that his head reares
Close to the Palme that Inops' fluent cheares.
    How shall I praise thee, farre being worthiest praise,
O Phœbus, to whose worth the law of layes                    30
In all kindes is ascrib'de? If feeding flocks

[57]

By Continent or Ile, all eminen'st rocks
Did sing for joy, Hill-tops, and floods in song
Did breake their billows, as they flow'd along
To serve the sea. The shores, the seas, and all                    35
Did sing as soone as from the lap did fall
Of blest Latona thee, the joy of Man.
Her Child-bed made the mountaine Cynthian
In rockie Delos, the sea-circled Ile,
On whose all sides the black seas brake their Pile                 40
And over-flowd for joy, so franck a Gale
The singing winds did on their waves exhale.

   Here borne, all mortalls live in thy commands, ⎫
Who ever Crete holds, Athens, or the strands       ⎬
Of th'Ile Ægina, or the famous lands           ⎭        45
For ships, Eubœa, or Eresia,
Or Peparethus, bordring on the sea,
Ægas, or Athos, that doth Thrace divide
And Macedon, or Pelion, with the pride
Of his high forehead, or the Samian Ile,                           50
That likewise lies neare Thrace, or Scyrus' soile,
Ida's steepe tops, or all that Phocis fill,
Or Autocanes, with the heaven-high hill,
Or populous Imber, Lemnos without Ports,
Or Lesbos, fit for the divine resorts,                             55
And sacred soile of blest Æolion;
Or Chius that exceeds comparison
For fruitfulnes, with all the Iles that lie
Embrac't with seas, Mimas, with rocks so hie,
Or Loftie-crownd Corycius, or the bright                           60
Charos, or Æsagæus' dazeling height,
Or waterie Samos; Mycale, that beares
Her browes even with the circles of the spheares,
Miletus, Cous, that the Citie is

Of voice-divided-choice humanities,                                        65
High Cnidus, Carpathus, still strooke with winde,
Naxus, and Paros, and the rockie-min'd
Rugged Rhenæa. Yet through all these parts,
Latona, great-growne with the King of darts,
Travailde, and tried if any would become                                   70
To her deare birth an hospitable home—
All which extremely trembled (shooke with feare),
Nor durst endure so high a birth to beare
In their free States, though, for it, they became
Never so fruitfull; till the reverend Dame                                 75
Ascended Delos, and her soile did sease
With these wing'd words: "O Delost would'st thou please
To be my sonne Apolloe's native seat,
And build a welthie Phane to one so great,
No one shall blame or question thy kinde deede. ⎫                           80
Nor think I, thou dost Sheepe or Oxen feede   ⎬
In any such store, or in vines exceede,       ⎭
Nor bring'st forth such innumerable Plants
(Which often make the rich Inhabitants
Careles of Deitie). If thou then should'st rere                            85
A Phane to Phœbus, all men would confer
Whole Hecatombs of beeves for sacrifice,
Still thronging hither. And to thee would rise
Ever unmeasur'd Odors, should'st thou long
Nourish thy King thus; and from forreigne wrong                            90
The Gods would guard thee, which thine owne addresse
Can never compasse for thy barrennesse."
   She said, and Delos joi'd, replying thus:
"Most happie sister of Saturnius!
I gladly would with all meanes entertein       ⎫                           95
The King your sonne, being now despis'de of men, ⎬
But should be honord with the greatest then.   ⎭

Yet this I feare, nor will conceale from thee:
Your Sonne (some say) will author miserie
In many kindes, as being to sustein                    100
A mightie empire over Gods and Men
Upon the holie-gift-giver, the earth.
And bitterly I feare that, when his birth
Gives him the sight of my so barren soile,
He will contemne, and give me up to spoile,            105
Enforce the sea to me, that ever will
Oppresse my heart with many a watrie hill.
And therefore let him chuse some other land,
Where he shall please to build at his command
Temple and Grove, set thick with many a Tree.         110
For wretched Polypusses breed in me
Retyring chambers, and black sea-calves Den
In my poore soile, for penurie of Men.
And yet, O Goddesse, would'st thou please to sweare
The Gods' great oath to me, before thou beare         115
Thy blessed Sonne here, that thou wilt erect
A Phane to him, to render the effect
Of men's demands to them before they fall,  ⎫
Then will thy sonne's renowne be generall,  ⎬
Men will his name in such varietie call,    ⎭
                                                       120
And I shall, then, be glad his birth to beare."         ⎫
    This said, the Gods' great oath she thus did swere: ⎬
"Know this, O earth! broad heaven's inferior sphere!    ⎭
And of blacke Styx the most infernall lake!—
Which is the gravest oath the Gods can take—           125
That here shall ever rise to Phœbus' Name
An odorous Phane and Altar; and thy fame
Honor, past all Iles else, shall see him emploid."
    Her oath thus tooke and ended, Delos joi'd
In mightie measure that she should become              130

To farr-shot Phœbus' birth the famous home.
  Latona then nine daies and nights did fall
In hopeles labor; at whose birth were all
Heaven's most supreame and worthie Goddesses,
Dione, Rhea, and th'Exploratresse                    135
Themis, and Amphitrite, that will be
Pursu'd with sighs still—every Deitie
Except the snowie-wristed wife of Jove,
Who held her moodes aloft, and would, not move.
Onely Lucina (to whose virtue vowes          )        140
Each Child-birth patient) heard not of her throwes, }
But sat (by Juno's counsaile) on the browes   )
Of broad Olympus, wrapt in clouds of gold;
Whom Jove's proud wife in envie did with-hold,
Because bright-lockt Latona was to beare              145
A Sonne so faultles and in force so cleare.
The rest Thaumantia sent before to bring
Lucina to release the envied King,
Assuring her that they would strait confer
A Carquenet, nine cubits long, on her,               150
All woven with wires of Gold. But chargd her, then,
To call apart from th'Ivorie-wristed Queene
The child-birth-guiding Goddesse, for just feare
Lest, her charge utter'd in Saturnia's eare,
She, after, might disswade her from descent.  )        155
  When winde-swift-footed Iris knew th'intent }
Of th'other Goddesses, away she went,        )
And instantly she past the infinite space
Twixt Earth and Heaven; when, comming to the place
Where dwelt th'Immortals, strait without the gate      160
She gat Lucina, and did all relate
The Goddesses commanded, and enclin'd
To all that they demanded her deare Minde.

And on their way they went, like those two Doves
That, walking high-waies, every shadow moves     165
Up from the earth, forc't with their naturall feare:
When entring Delos, she that is so deare
To Dames in labor made Latona strait
Prone to deliverie, and to weild the wait
Of her deare burthen with a world of ease.     170
When with her faire hand she a Palme did sease,
And (staying her by it) stucke her tender knees
Amidst the soft meade, that did smile beneath
Her sacred labor; and the child did breath
The aire in th'instant. All the Goddesses     175
Brake in kinde teares and shrikes for her quicke ease,
And Thee, O Archer Phœbus, with waves cleere
Washt sweetly over, swadled with sincere
And spotlesse swath-bands; and made then to flow
About thy breast a mantle, white as snow,     180
Fine, and new made; and cast a Veile of Gold
Over thy forehead. Nor yet forth did hold
Thy mother for thy foode her golden brest,
But Themis, in supply of it, addrest
Lovely Ambrosia, and drunke off to thee     185
A Bowie of Nectar, interchangeablie
With her immortall fingers serving thine.
And when, O Phœbus, that eternall wine
Thy tast had relisht, and that foode divine,
No golden swath-band longer could containe     190
Thy panting bosome; all that would constraine
Thy soone-easd God-head, every feeble chaine
Of earthy Child-rights, flew in sunder all.
And then didst thou thus to the Deities call:
    "Let there be given me my lov'd Lute and Bow;     195
I'le prophecie to men, and make them know

Jove's perfect counsailes." This said, up did flie
From brode-waide Earth the unshorne Deitie,
Far-shot Apollo. All th'Immortalls stood
In steepe amaze to see Latonae's brood.                    200
All Delos, looking on him, all with gold
Was loden strait, and joi'd to be extold
By great Latona so, that she decreed
Her barrennesse should beare the fruitfulst seed
Of all the Iles and Continents of earth,                   205
And lov'd her from her heart so for her birth.
For so she florisht as a hill that stood
Crownd with the flowre of an abundant wood:
And thou, O Phœbus, bearing in thy hand
Thy silver bow, walk'st over every land,                   210
Sometimes ascend'st the rough-hewne rockie hill
Of desolate Cynthus, and sometimes tak'st will
To visit Ilands, and the Plumps of men.
And manie a Temple, all wayes, men ordein
To thy bright God-head; Groves, made darke with Trees,     215
And never shorne, to hide ye Deities,
All high-lov'd Prospects, all the steepest browes
Of farr-seene Hills, and every flood that flowes
Forth to the sea, are dedicate to Thee.
But most of all thy minde's Alacritie                      220
Is rais'd with Delos; since to fill thy Phane
There flocks so manie an Ionian,
With ample Gownes that flowe downe to their feet,
With all their children, and the reverend Sweet
Of all their pious wives. And these are they               225
That (mindefull of thee) even thy Deitie
Render more spritelie with their Champion fight,
Dances, and songs, perform'd to glorious sight,
Once having publisht and proclaim'd their strife.

And these are acted with such exquisite life                     230
That one would say, "Now, the Ionian straines
Are turn'd Immortalls, nor know what Age meanes."
His minde would take such pleasure from his eye,
To see them serv'd by all Mortalitie,
Their men so humane, women so well-grac't,                       235
Their ships so swift, their riches so encreast,
Since thy observance, who (being all before
Thy opposites) were all despis'd and poore.
And to all these this absolute wonder add,
Whose praise shall render all posterities gladd:                 240
The Delian Virgines are thy handmaides, All,
And, since they serv'd Apollo, jointly fall
Before Latona, and Diana too,
In sacred service, and doe therefore know
How to make mention of the ancient Trimms                        245
Of men and women in their well-made Hymns,
And soften barbarous Nations with their songs,
Being able, all, to speake the severall tongu's
Of forreine Nations, and to imitate
Their musiques there, with art so fortunate                      250
That one would say, there every one did speake,
And all their tunes in naturall accents breake,
Their songs so well compos'd are, and their Art
To answer all soundes is of such Desart.
       But come, Latona, and thou king of Flames,                255
With Phœbe, Rectresse of chaste thoughts in Dames,
Let me salute ye, and your Graces call
Hereafter to my just memoriall.
       And you, O Delian Virgins, doe me grace,  ⎫
When any stranger of our earthie Race            ⎬               260
Whose restlesse life Affliction hath in chace  ⎭
Shall hither come and question you: "Who is,

To your chaste eares, of choicest faculties
In sacred Poesie, and with most right
Is Author of your absolut'st delight?"                    265
Ye shall your selves doe all the right ye can
To answer for our Name: "The sightlesse man
Of stonie Chios. All whose Poems shall
In all last Ages stand for Capitall."
This for your owne sakes I desire; for I                  270
Will propagate mine owne precedencie
As far as earth shall well-built cities beare,
Or humane conversation is held deare—
Not with my praise direct, but praises due,
And men shall credit it because tis true.                 275
   How ever, I'le not cease the praise I vow
To farre-shot Phœbus with the silver bow,
Whom lovely-hair'd Latona gave the light.
O King! both Lycia is in Rule thy Right,
Faire Mœonie, and the Maritimall                          280
Miletus, wisht to be the seate of all.
   But chiefely Delos, girt with billowes round,
Thy most respected empire doth resound—
Where thou to Pythus wentst, to answer there
(As soone as thou wert borne) the burning eare            285
Of many a far-come to heare future deeds,
Clad in divine and odoriferous weeds,
And with thy Golden Fescue plaidst upon
Thy hollow Harp, that sounds to heaven set gone.
   Then to Olympus swift as thought hee flew           290
To Jove's high house, and had a retinew
Of Gods t'attend him. And then strait did fall
To studie of the Harp and Harpsicall
All th'Immortalls. To whom every Muse
With ravishing voices did their answers use,              295

[65]

Singing th'eternall deeds of Deitie,
And from their hands what Hells of miserie
Poore Humanes suffer, living desperate quite, ⎫
And not an Art they have, wit, or deceipt, ⎬
Can make them manage any Act aright, ⎭          300
Nor finde, with all the soule they can engage,
A salve for Death, or remedie for Age.

But here the fayre-hayrd graces, the wise Howres,
Harmonia, Hebe, and sweet Venus' powres,
Danc't, and each other's Palme to Palme did cling, ⎫
And with these danc't not a deformed thing, ⎬
No forspoke Dwarfe, nor downeward witherling, ⎭
But all with wondrous goodly formes were deckt,
And mov'd with Beauties of unpris'd aspect.

Dart-deare-Diana (even with Phœbus bred)          310
Danc't likewise there; and Mars a march did tred
With that brave Bevie. In whose consort fell
Argicides, th'ingenious Sentinell.
Phœbus-Apollo toucht his Lute to them
Sweetely and softly, a most glorious beame          315
Casting about him as he danc't and plaid,
And even his feet were all with raies araide.
His weede and all, of a most curious Trymm,
With no lesse Luster grac't and circled him.

By these Latona, with a hayre that shin'd          320
Like burnisht gold, and (with the Mightie Minde)
Heaven's Counsailor, Jove, sat with delightsome eyes,
To see their Sonne new rankt with Deities.

How shall I praise thee, then, that art all praise?
Amongst the Brides shall I thy Deitie raise?          325
Or being in love, when, sad, thou wentst to wowe
The Virgin Aza, and didst overthrowe
The even-with-Gods, Elation's Mightie seed,

That had of goodly horse so brave a breed,
And Phorbas, sonne of soveraigne Triopus,                    330
Valiant Leucippus, and Ereutheus,
And Triopus himselfe, with equall fall,
Thou but on foot, and they on horsebacke all?
   Or shall I sing thee, as thou first didst grace
Earth with thy foot, to finde thee forth a place              335
Fit to pronounce thy Oracles to Men?
First from Olympus thou alightedst then
Into Pieria, passing all the land
Of fruitles Lesbos, chok't with drifts of sand,
The Magnets likewise, and the Perrhæbes;                     340
And to Iolcus variedst thy accesse,
Cenæus' Topps ascending, that their Base
Make bright Eubœa, being of ships the Grace,
And fixt thy faire stand in Lelantus' field,
That did not yet thy minde's Contentment yeeld                345
To raise a Phane on, and a sacred Grove.
   Passing Euripus then, thou mad'st remove
Up to earth's ever-greene and holyest Hill,
Yet swiftly thence, too, thou transcendedst still
To Mycalessus, and did'st touch upon                          350
Teumessus, apt to make greene couches on,
And flowrie field-bedds. Then thy Progresse found
Thebes out, whose soile with onely woods was crown'd.
For yet was sacred Thebes no humane seate, ⎫
And therefore were no Paths nor high waies beat ⎬            355
On her free bosome, that flowes now with wheat, ⎭
But then she onely wore on it a wood.
   From hence (even loth to part, because it stood
Fit for thy service) thou put'st on Remove
To greene Onchestus, Neptune's glorious Grove,               360
Where new-tam'd horse, bredd, nourish nerves so rare

That still they frolick, though they travaild are
Never so sore, and hurrie after them
Most heavie Coches, but are so extream
(In usuall-travaile) fierie-and-free                              365
That, though their cochman ne're so masterlie
Governes their courages, he sometimes must
Forsake his seat, and give their spirits their lust—
When after them their emptie coach they drawe,
Foming and Neighing, quite exempt from awe.                       370
And if their Cocheman guide through any Grove
Unshorne, and vow'd to any Deitie's Love,
The Lords encocht leap out, and all their care
Use to allaie their fires, with speaking faire,
Stroking and trimming them, and in some queach                   375
(Or strength of shade) within their nearest reach
Reigning them up, invoke the deified King
Of that unshorne and everlasting spring,
And leave them then to her preserving hands
Who is the Fate that there the God commands.                     380
And this was first the sacred fashion there.
From hence thou wentst, O thou in shafts past Pere,
And found'st Cephissus with thy all-seeing beames,
Whose flood affects so many silver streames,
And from Lilæus poures so bright a wave.                         385
     Yet forth thy foot flew, and thy faire eyes gave
The view of Ocale, the rich in towrs;
Then to Amartus, that abounds in flowrs,
Then to Delphusa putt'st thy progresse on,
Whose blessed soile nought harmefull breeds upon.                390
And there thy pleasure would a Phane adorne,
And nourish woods whose shades should ne're be shorne.
Where this thou told'st her, standing to her close:
"Delphusa, here I entertaine suppose

To build a farr-fam'd Temple, and ordein                      395
An Oracle t'informe the mindes of Men,
Who shall for ever offer to my love
Whole Hecatombs—even all the men that move
In rich Peloponnesus, and all those
Of Europe, and the Iles the seas enclose,                     400
Whom future search of Acts and Beings brings— ⎫
To whom I'le prophecie the truths of things      ⎬
In that rich Temple where my Oracle sings."       ⎭
    This said, the all-bounds-reacher with his bowe
The Phane's divine foundations did foreshowe;                 405
Ample they were, and did huge length impart,
With a continuate Tenour, full of Art.
But when Delphusa look't into his end,
Her heart grew angrie, and did thus extend
It selfe to Phœbus: "Phœbus, since thy minde                  410
A farr-fam'd Phane hath in it selfe design'd
To beare an Oracle to men in me,
That Hecatombs may put in fire to thee,
This let me tell thee, and impose for staie  ⎫
Upon thy purpose: th'Inarticulate neye       ⎬                415
Of fire-hov'd horse will ever disobaie         ⎭
Thy numerous eare, and mules will for their drinke
Trouble my sacred springs, and I should thinke
That any of the humane Race had rather
See here the hurreys of rich Coches gather,                   420
And heare the haughtie Neys of swift-hov'd horse,
Than (in his pleasure's place) convert recourse
T'a Mightie Temple; and his wealth bestow  ⎫
On Pieties, where his sports may freely flow, ⎬
Or see huge wealth that he shall never owe.  ⎭                425
And therefore (wouldst thou heare my free advise,
Though Mightier farre thou art, and much more wise,

O King, than I, thy powre being great'st of all),
In Crissa, underneath the bosome's fall
Of steepe Parnassus, let thy minde be given                      430
To set thee up a Phane, where never driven
Shall glorious Coches be, nor horses' Neys
Storme neare thy well-built Altars, but thy praise
Let the faire race of pious Humanes bring
Into thy Phane, that Io-Pæans sing.                              435
And those gifts onely let thy Deified minde      ⎫
Be circularlie pleas'd with, being the kinde      ⎬
And fayre-burnt-offrings that true Deities binde."  ⎭
With this, his minde she altered, though she spake
Not for his good, but her owne glorie's sake.                    440
   From hence, O Phœbus, first thou mad'st retreat,
And of the Phlegians reacht the walled seat,
Inhabited with contumelious Men,
Whoe, sleighting Jove, tooke up their dwellings then
Within a large Cave neare Cephissus' Lake.                       445
Hence, swiftly moving, thou all speed didst make
Up to the tops intended, and the ground
Of Crissa, under the with-snowe-still-croun'd
Parnassus, reacht, whose face affects the west;
Above which hangs a rock that still seemes prest                 450
To fall upon it, through whose brest doth runn
A rockie Cave, neare which the King the Sunn
Cast to contrive a Temple to his minde,
And said: "Now heere stands my conceipt inclin'd
To build a famous Phane, where still shall be                    455
An Oracle to Men, that still to me.
Shall offer absolute Hecatombs, as well
Those that in rich Peloponnesus dwell
As those of Europe, and the Iles that lie
Walld with the sea, that all their paines applie                 460

T'employ my counsailes. To all which will I
True secrets tell, by way of Prophesie,
In my rich Temple, that shall ever be
An Oracle to all Posteritie."
This said, the Phane's forme he did strait present,            465
Ample, and of a length of great extent;
In which Trophonius and Agamede
(Who of Erginus were the famous seed)
Impos'd the stonie Entrie, and the Heart
Of every God had for their excellent Art.                     470
    About the Temple dwelt of humane Name
Unnumbred Nations, it acquir'd such Fame,
Being all of stone, built for eternall date.
And neare it did a Fountaine propagate
A fayre streame farr away; when Jove's, bright seed,          475
The King Apollo, with an arrow, freed
From his strong string, destroid the Dragonesse
That Wonder nourisht, being of such excesse
In size and horridnesse of monstrous shape,
That on the forc't earth she wrought many a rape,            480
Many a spoile made on it, many an ill
On crooke-hancht Herds brought, being impurpl'd still
With blood of all sorts; having undergone
The charge of Juno, with the golden Throne,
To nourish Typhon, the abhorr'd affright                      485
And bane of mortals—whom into the light
Saturnia brought forth, being incenst with Jove,
Because the most renowm'd fruit of his love,
Pallas, he got, and shooke out of his braine.
For which Majestique Juno did complaine                       490
In this kinde to the blest Court of the skies:
"Know all ye sex-distinguisht Deities,
That Jove (assembler of the cloudie throng)

Beginns with me first and affects with wrong
My right in him, made by himselfe his wife,                495
That knowes and does the honor'd marriage life
All honest offices; and yet hath he            ⎫
Undulie got, without my companie,             ⎬
Blew-eyd Minerva, who of all the skie          ⎭
Of blest Immortalls is the absolute Grace;                500
Where I have brought into the heavenly Race
A Sonne, both taken in his feet and head
So oughly, and so farr from worth my bedd,
That (ravisht into hand) I tooke and threw
Downe to the vast sea his detested view;                  505
Where Nereus' Daughter, Thetis, who her waie
With silver feet makes, and the faire araie
'Of her bright sisters sav'd, and tooke to guard.
But would to heaven, another yet were spar'd
The like Grace of his God-head. Craftie mate,             510
What other scape canst thou excogitate?
How could thy heart sustaine to get alone
The grey-eyd Goddesse? Her conception
Nor bringing forth had any hand of mine,
And yet know all the Gods I goe for thine                 515
To such kinde uses. But I'le now employ
My braine to procreate a masculine Joy,
That 'mongst th'Immortalls may as eminent shine,
With shame affecting nor my bedd nor thine.
Nor will I ever touch at thine againe,                    520
But farr fly it and thee; and yet will raigne
Amongst th'Immortalls ever." This spleene spent,
(Still yet left angrie) farre away she went
From all the Deathlesse, and yet praid to all,
Advanc't her hand, and e're she let it fall               525
Us'd these excitements: "Heare me now, O Earth!

Brode Heaven above it, and beneath, your birth,
The Deified Titanois, that dwell about
Vast Tartarus, from whence sprung all the Rout
Of Men and Deities! Heare me all, I say,                    530
With all your forces, and give instant way
T'a sonne of mine, without Jove, who yet may
Nothing inferiour prove in force to him,
But past him spring as farre in able lim
As he past Saturne." This pronounc't, she strooke           535
Life-bearing Earth so strongly, that she shooke
Beneath her numb'd hand—which when she beheld,
Her bosome with abundant comforts sweld,
In hope all should to her desire extend.
From hence the Yeare that all such proofes gives end        540
Grew round; yet all that time the bed of Jove
Shee never toucht at, never was her love
Enflam'd to sit nere his Dædalian Throne,
As she accustomed, to consult upon
Counsells kept darke with many a secret skill,              545
But kept her Vow-frequented Temple still,
Pleas'd with her sacrifice; till now, the Nights
And Daies accomplish't, and the yeare's whole rights
In all her revolutions being expir'de,
The Howres, and all, run out that were requir'd             550
To vent a Birth-right, she brought forth a Sonne,
Like Gods or Men in no condition,
But a most dreadfull and pernicious thing
Call'd Typhon, who on all the humane Spring
Confer'd confusion—which receiv'd to hand                   555
By Juno, instantly she gave command
(Ill to ill adding) that the Dragonesse
Should bring it up; who tooke, and did oppresse
With many a misery (to maintaine th'excesse

Of that inhumane Monster) all the Race                           560
Of Men that were of all the world the grace—
Till the farre-working Phœbus at her sent
A fierie Arrow, that invok't event
Of death gave to her execrable life.
Before which yet she lay in bitter strife,                       565
With dying paines groveling on earth, and drew ⎱
Extreme short respirations; for which flew       ⎰
A shout about the aire, whence no man knew ⎭
But came by power divine. And then she lay
Tumbling her Truncke, and winding every way                      570
About her nastie Nest, quite leaving then
Her murtherous life, embru'd with deaths of Men.
    Then Phœbus gloried, saying: "Thy selfe now lie
On Men-sustaining Earth, and putrifie,
Who first of Putrifaction was inform'd.                          575
Now on thy life have Death's cold vapors stormd,
That stormd'st on Men the Earth-fed so much death,
In envie of the Of-spring they made breathe
Their lives out on my Altars. Now from thee
Not Typhon shall enforce the miserie                             580
Of merited death, nor shee whose name implies ⎱
Such scath, Chimæra, but blacke earth make prise ⎰
To putrifaction thy Immanities,               ⎭
And bright Hyperion, that light all eyes showes,
Thyne with a night of rottennesse shall close."                 585
    Thus spake he glory'ng; and then seas'd upon
Her horrid heape, with Putrifaction,
Hyperion's lovely powrs; from whence her name
Tooke sound of Python, and heaven's soveraigne flame
Was surnam'd Pythius, since the sharp-eyd Sunn                   590
Affected so with Putrifaction

The hellish Monster. And now Phœbus' minde
Gave him to know that falsehood had strooke blinde
Even his bright eye, because it could not finde
The subtle Fountaine's fraud—to whom he flew,          595
Enflam'd with anger, and in th'instant drew
Close to Delphusa, using this short vow:
  "Delphusa! you must looke no longer now
To vent your frauds on me; for well I know
Your scituation to be lovely worth          600
A Temple's Imposition, it poures forth
So delicate a streame. But your renowne
Shall now no longer shine here, but mine owne."
  This said, he thrust her Promontorie downe,
And damn'd her fountaine up with mightie stones,          605
A Temple giving consecrations
In woods adjoining. And in this Phane all
On him, by surname of Delphusius, call,
Because Delphusa's sacred flood and fame
His wrath affected so, and hid in shame.          610
  And then thought Phœbus what descent of Men
To be his Ministers he should retein,
To doe in stonie Pythos sacrifice.
To which his minde contending, his quicke eies
He cast upon the blew Sea, and beheld          615
A ship, on whose Masts sailes that wing'd it sweld,
In which were men transferr'd, many and good,
That in Minoian Cnossus eate their food,
And were Cretensians; who now are those
That all the sacrifising dues dispose,          620
And all the lawes deliver to a word
Of Daie's great King, that weares the golden sword,
And Oracles (out of his Delphian Tree

That shrowds her faire armes in the Cavitie
Beneath Parnassus' Mount) pronounce to Men.                    625
These, now his Priests, that liv'd as Merchants then,
In trafficks and Pecuniarie Rates
For sandie Pylos and the Pylian States
Were under saile. But now encounterd them
Phœbus Apollo, who into the streame                            630
Cast himselfe headlong, and the strange disguise
Tooke of a Dolphine of a goodly sise—
Like which He leapt into their ship, and lay
As an Ostent of infinite dismay,
For none with any strife of Minde could looke ⎞                635
Into the Omen. All the shipmasts shooke,         ⎬
And silent all sate with the feare they tooke,   ⎠
Armd not, nor strooke they saile, but as before
Went on with full Trim; and a foreright Blore,
Stiff and from forth the South, the ship made flie.            640
When first they stript the Malean Promont'rie,
Toucht at Laconia's soile, in which a Towne
Their ship ariv'd at, that the Sea doth Crowne,
Call'd Tenarus, a place of much delight
To men that serve Heaven's Comforter of sight,                 645
In which are fed the famous flocks that beare
The wealthie Fleeces, on a delicate Laire
Being fed, and seated—where the Merchants faine
Would have put in, that they might out againe
To tell the Miracle that chanc't to them,                      650
And trie if it would take the sacred streame,
Rushing far forth, that he againe might beare
Those other Fishes that abounded there
Delightsome companie, or still would stay
Abord their drie ship. But it failde t'obay,                   655
And for the rich Peloponnesian shore

Steer'de her free saile; Apollo made the Blore
Directly guide it. That, obaying still,
Reacht drie Arena, and (what wish doth fill)
Faire Argyphæa, and the populous height          660
Of Thryus, whose streame (siding her) doth weight
With safe passe on Alphæus, Pylos' sands
And Pylian dwellers; keeping by the strands
On which th'Inhabitants of Crunius dwell,
And Helida, set opposite to Hell;                665
Chalcis and Dymes reach't, and happily
Made saile by Pheras—all being over-joide
With that francke Gale that Jove himselfe emploid.
And then amongst the cloudes they might descrie
The Hill that far-seene Ithaca calls her Eie,     670
Dulichius, Samos, and, with timber grac't,
Shadie Zacynthus. But when now they past
Peloponnesus all, and then when show'de
The infinite Vale of Crissa, that doth shroud
All rich Morea with her liberall brest,           675
So francke a Gale there flew out of the West
As all the skie discovered; twas so great,
And blew so from the verie Counsell seat
Of Jove himselfe, that quickly it might send
The ship through full Seas to her journey's end.  680
    From thence they saild, quite opposite, to the East,
And to the Region where light leaves his rest,
The Light himselfe being sacred Pylot there,
And made the Sea-trod ship arive them nere
The Grapefull Crissa, where he rest doth take     685
Close to her Port and sands. And then forth brake
The far-shot King, like to a starre that strowes
His glorious forehead where the Mid-day glowes,
That all in sparkles did his state attire,

[77]

Whose Luster leapt up to the spheare of fire.                690
He trodd where no waie op'te, and pierst the place
That of his sacred Tripods held the grace,
In which he lighted such a fluent flame
As guilt all Crissa; in which every Dame
And Dame's faire daughter cast out vehement cries          695
At those fell fires of Phœbus' Prodigies,
That shaking feares through all their fancies threw.
Then (like the minde's swift light) againe he flew
Backe to the ship, shap't like a youth in Height
Of all his graces, shoulders broad and streit,             700
And all his haire in golden currls enwrapt;
And to the Merchants thus his speech he shap't:
    "Ho! strangers! what are you? and from what seat
Saile ye these waies that salt and water sweat?
To traffick justlie? or use vagrant scapes                 705
Voyde of all rule, conferring wrongs and Rapes
(Like Pyrats) on the men ye never sawe,
With mindes project, exempt from list or Lawe?
Why sit ye heere so stupified, nor take
Land while ye may, nor deposition make                     710
Of Navall Arms, when this the fashion is
Of men Industrious, who (their faculties
Wearied at sea) leave ship, and use the land
For foode, that with their healths and stomacks stand?"
    This said, with bold mindes he their brest suppli'd,    715
And thus made answer the Cretensian guide:
    "Stranger! because you seeme to us no seed
Of any mortall, but celestiall breed
For parts and person, Joy your steps ensue,
And Gods make good the blisse we thinke your due.           720
Vouchsafe us true relation, on what land
We here arive, and what men here command.

## An Hymne to Apollo

We were for well-knowne parts bound, and from Crete
(Our vanted countrie) to the Pylian seat
Vow'd our whole voyage. Yet arive we here,                    725
Quite crosse to those wills that our motions stere,
Wishing to make returne some other way,
Some other course desirous to assaie,
To pay our lost paines. But some God hath fill'd
Our frustrate sayles, defeating what we will'd."           730
   Apollo answerd: "Strangers! though before
Yee dwelt in wooddie Cnossus, yet no more
Yee must be made your owne Reciprocalls
To your lov'd Cittie and faire severalls
Of wives and houses. But ye shall have here                  735
My wealthie Temple, honord farre and nere
Of many a Nation; for my selfe am Son
To Jove himselfe, and of Apollo won
The glorious Title, who thus safelie through
The sea's vast billows still have held your plough,          740
No ill intending, that will let ye make
My Temple here your owne, and honors take
Upon your selves, all that to me are given.
And more, the counsailes of the King of Heaven
Your selves shall know, and with his will receive           745
Ever the honors that all men shall give.
Doe as I say then instantly: strike saile,
Take downe your Tackling, and your vessell hale
Up into land; your goods bring forth, and all
The instruments that into sayling fall;                     750
Make on this shore an Altar, fire enflame,
And barley white cakes-offer to my name.
And then (environing the Altar) pray, ⎫
And call me (as ye sawe me in the day ⎬
When from the windie seas I brake swift way ⎭                755

Into your ship) Delphinius, since I tooke
A Dolphin's forme then. And to every looke
That there shall seeke it, that my Altar shall
Be made a Delphian memoriall
From thence for ever. After this, ascend 760
Your swift black ship and sup, and then intend
Ingenuous Offerings to the equall Gods
That in celestiall seates make blest abods—
When (having staid your helthfull hunger's sting)
Come all with me, and Io-Pæans sing 765
All the waie's length, till you attaine the state
Where I your oppulent Phane have consecrate."

    To this they gave him passing diligent eare,
And vow'd to his obedience all they were.

    First, striking sayle, their tacklings then they los'd, 770
And (with their Gables stoop't) their mast impos'd
Into the Mast roome. Forth themselves then went,
And from the sea into the Continent
Drew up their ship, which farr up from the sand
They rais'd with ample rafters. Then in hand 775
They tooke the Altar, and inform'd it on
The sea's nere shore, imposing thereupon
White cakes of barley, fire made, and did stand
About it round, as Phœbus gave command,
Submitting Invocations to his will; 780
Then sacrifis'd to all the heavenly Hill
Of powrefull God-heads. After which they eat
Abord their ship, till with fit food repleat
They rose, nor to their Temple us'd delay.
Whom Phœbus usherd, and toucht all the way 785
His heavenly Lute with Art above admir'd,
Gracefully leading them. When all were fir'd
With zeale to him, and follow'd wondring, all,

To Pythos; and upon his name did call
With Io-Pæans, such as Cretans use.         790
And in their bosomes did the deified Muse
Voices of honey-Harmonie infuse.
   With never-wearie feet their way they went,
And made with all alacritie ascent
Up to Parnassus, and that long'd-for place     795
Where they should live, and be of men the Grace.
When, all the way, Apollo shew'd them still
Their farr-stretcht valleys, and their two-topt Hill,
Their famous Phane, and all that all could raise
To a supreame height of their Joy, and praise.    800
   And then the Cretan Captaine thus enquir'd
Of King Apollo: "Since you have retir'd,
O Soveraigne, our sad lives so farr from friends
And native soile (because so farr extends
Your deare minde's pleasure) tell us how we shall    805
Live in your service. To which question call
Our provident mindes, because we see not croun'd
This soile with store of vines, nor doth abound
In welthie meddows, on which we may live,
As well as on men our attendance give."    810
   He smil'd, and said: "O men, that nothing know
And so are follow'd with a world of woe,
That needs will succour care and curious mone,
And poure out sighs without cessation,
Were all the riches of the earth your owne!    815
Without much busines, I will render knowne
To your simplicities an easie way
To wealth enough. Let every man purvaie
A skeane (or slaugh'ring steele) and his right hand
(Bravely bestowing) evermore see mann'd    820
With killing sheepe, that to my Phane will flowe

From all farr Nations. On all which bestowe
Good observation, and all else they give
To me make you your owne all, and so live.
For all which watch before my Temple well,                    825
And all my counsailes, above all, conceale.
If any give vaine language, or to deeds,
Yea, or as farr as injurie proceedes,
Know that (at losers' hands) for those that gaine,
It is the lawes of Mortalls to sustaine.                       830
Besides, yee shall have Princes to obay,
Which still yee must, and (so yee gaine) yee may.
All, now, is said; give all thy memorie's stay."
    And thus to thee, Jove and Latona's Sonne,
Be given all grace of salutation.                              835
Both thee and others of th'Immortall state
My song shall memorize to endlesse date.

*THE END OF THE HYMNE TO APOLLO*

## A HYMNE TO HERMES

Hermes, the Sonne of Jove and Maia, sing,
O Muse, th'Arcadian and Cyllenian King,
They rich in flocks, he heaven enriching still
In Messages return'd with all his will—
Whom glorious Maia, the Nimph rich in haire,                5
Mixing with Jove in amorous affaire,
Brought forth to him, sustaining a retreat
From all th'Immortalls of the blessed seat,
And living in the same darke Cave where Jove
Inform'd at mid-night the effect of love,                   10
Unknowne to either man or Deitie,
Sweet sleepe once having seas'd the jelous eye
Of Juno, deckt with wrists of ivorie.
But when great Jove's high minde was consummate,
The tenth moneth had in heaven confin'de the date          15
Of Maia's Labour, and into the sight
She brought, in one birth, Labours infinite:
For then she bore a sonne, that all tried waies
Could turne and winde to wisht events assaies,
A faire tongu'd, but false-hearted, Counsellor,            20
Rector of Ox-stealers, and for all stealths bore
A varied finger; Speeder of Night's spies
And guide of all her dreames' obscurities;
Guard of dore-Guardians; and was borne to be
Amongst th'Immortalls that wing'd Deitie                   25
That in an instant should doe acts would aske
The Powres of others an Eternall Taske.
Borne in the Morne, he form'd his Lute at Noone,
At Night stole all the Oxen of the Sunne;
And all this in his Birth's first day was done,            30
Which was the fourth of the encreasing Moone.

Because Celestiall lims sustain'd his straines,
His sacred swath-bands must not be his chaines.
So (starting up) to Phœbus' Herde he stept,
Found strait the high-rooft Cave where they were kept,     35
And (th'entrie passing) he th'invention found
Of making Lutes; and did in wealth abound
By that Invention, since he first of all
Was author of that Engine Musicall,
By this meane mov'd to the ingenious worke:                40
Nere the Cave's inmost overture did lurke
A Tortois, tasting th'odoriferous grasse,
Leisurely moving; and this Object was
The motive to Jove's Sonne (who could convert
To profitablest uses all desert                            45
That nature had in any worke convaid)
To forme the Lute; when (smiling) thus he said:
"Thou mov'st in me a note of excellent use,
Which thy ill forme shall never so seduce
T'evert the good to be inform'd by it,                     50
In pliant force of my forme-forging wit."
    Then the slowe Tortois, wrought on by his minde,
He thus saluted: "All joy to the kinde
Instinct of nature in thee, borne to be
The spirriter of Dances, companie                          55
For feasts and following Banquets, grac't and blest
For bearing light to all the interest
Claim'd in this Instrument—from whence shall spring
Play faire and sweet, to which may Graces sing.
A prettie painted cote thou putt'st on here,               60
O Tortois, while thy hill-bred vitall sphere
Confines thy fashion; but (surpris'd by me)
I'le beare thee home, where thou shalt ever be
A Profit to me; and yet nothing more

Will I contemne thee in my merited store.                    65
Goods, with good parts got, worth and honour gave;
Left goods and honors every foole may have.
And since thou first shalt give me meanes to live,
I'le love thee ever. Virtuous qualities give
To live at home with them enough content,                    70
Where those that want such inward ornament
Fly out for outward, their life made their lode:
*Tis best to be at home; Harme lurks abroad.*
And certainely thy vertue shall be knowne
Gainst great-yll-causing incantation                         75
To serve as for a Lance or Ammulet.
And where, in comfort of thy vitall heat,
Thou now breathst but a sound confus'd for song.
Expos'd by nature, after death, more strong
Thou shalt in sounds of Art be, and command                  80
Song infinite sweeter." Thus with either hand
He tooke it up, and instantly tooke flight
Back to his Cave with that his home-delight—
Where (giving to the Mountaine Tortois vents
Of life and motion) with fit Instruments                     85
Forg'd of bright steele he strait inform'd a Lute,
Put neck and frets to it, of which a sute
He made of splitted quills, in equall space
Impos'd upon the neck, and did embrace
Both backe and bosome. At whose height (as gynns             90
T'extend and ease the strings) he put in pynns.
Seven strings, of severall tunes, he then applied,
Made of the Entrailes of a sheepe well dried,
And throughly twisted. Next he did provide
A Case for all, made of an Oxe's Hyde,                        95
Out of his counsailes to preserve as well
As to create. And all this Action fell

Into an instant consequence. His word
And worke had individuall accord,
All being as swiftly to perfection brought                    100
As any worldly man's most ravisht thought,
Whose minde Care cuts in an infinity ⎫
Of varied parts or passions instantly, ⎬
Or as the frequent twincklings of an eye. ⎭
    And thus his House-delight given absolute end,            105
He toucht it, and did every string extend
(With an exploratorie spirit assaid)
To all the parts that could on it be plaid.
It sounded dreadfully; to which he sung,
As if from thence the first and true force sprung            110
That fashions Virtue. God in him did sing.
His play was likewise an unspeakable thing,
Yet, but as an extemporall Assay
Of what showe it would make, being the first way,
It tryed his hand; or a tumultuous noise                     115
Such as at feasts the first-flowr'd spirits of Boies
Poure out in mutuall contumelies still,
As little squaring with his curious will,
Or was as wanton and untaught a Store.
    Of Jove and Maia, that rich shooes still wore,            120
He sung; who sufferd ill reports before,
And foule staines under her faire titles bore.
But Hermes sung her Nation, and her Name
Did itterate ever—all her high-flowne fame
Of being Jove's Mistresse; celebrating all                   125
Her traine of servants, and collaterall
Sumpture of Houses; all her Tripods there,
And Caldrons huge, encreasing every yeare.
All which she knew, yet felt her knowledge stung

With her fame's losse, which (found) she more wisht  
   sung.                                     130  
But now he in his sacred cradle laid  
His Lute so absolute, and strait convaid  
Himselfe up to a watch-towre forth his house,  
Rich and divinely Odoriferous,  
A loftie wile at worke in his conceipt,         135  
Thirsting the practise of his Empire's height.  
And where Impostors rule (since sable Night  
Must serve their deeds) he did his deeds their right—  
For now the never-resting Sunne was turn'd  
For th'under earth, and in the Ocean burn'd    140  
His Coch and Coursers. When th'ingenious spie  
Pieria's shadie hill had in his eye,  
Where the immortall Oxen of the Gods  
In ayre's flood solac't their select Abods,  
And earth's sweet greene floure, that was never shorne,  145  
Fed ever downe. And these the wittie-borne  
Argicides set serious spie upon,  
Severing from all the rest and setting gone  
Full fiftie of the violent Bellowers.  
Which driving through the sands, he did reverse    150  
(His birth's-craft strait remembring) all their hoves,  
And them transpos'd in opposite removes,  
The fore behinde set, the behinde before,  
T'employ the eyes of such as should explore.  
And he himselfe (as slye-pac't) cast away    155  
His sandalls on the sea-sands; past display  
And unexcogitable thoughts in Act  
Putting, to shunn of his stolne steps the Tract,  
Mixing both Tamrisk and like-Tamrisk sprayes  
In a most rare confusion, to raise    160

His footsteps up from earth. Of which sprayes he
(His armefull gathering fresh from off the Tree)
Made for his sandalls Tyes, both leaves and tyes
Holding together; and then fear'd no eyes
That could affect his feet's discoveries.                    165

    The Tamrisk boughs he gather'd, making way
Backe from Pieria, but as to convaie
Provision in them for his journey fit,
It being long and, therefore, needing it.

    An ould man, now at labour nere the field           170
Of greene Onchestus, knew the verdant yield
Of his fayre armefull; whom th'ingenious Sonne
Of Maia, therefore, salutation
Did thus beginn to: "Ho! ould man! that now
Art crooked growne with making Plants to grow,              175
Thy nerves will farr be spent, when these boughs shall
To these their leaves confer me fruit and All.
But see not thou what ever thou dost see,
Nor heare, though heare; but all as touching me
Conceale, since nought it can endamage thee."               180

    This and no more he said, and on drave still
His brode-browd Oxen. Many a shadie Hill,
And many an echoing valley, many a field
Pleasant and wishfull, did his passage yield
Their safe Transcension. But now the divine                 185
And black-browd Night (his Mistresse) did decline
Exceeding swiftly, Daie's most earely light
Fast hasting to her first point, to excite
Worldlings to worke; and in her Watch-towre shone
King Pallas-Megamedes' seed, the Moone;                     190
When through th'Alphæan flood Jove's powerfull Sonne
Phœbus-Apollo's ample-foreheaded Herd
(Whose necks the laboring yoke had never spher'd)

[88]

Drave swiftly on; and then into a stall
(Hillie, yet past to through an humble vale                    195
And hollow Dells, in a most lovely Meade)
He gatherd all, and them divinely fedd
With Odorous Cypresse and the ravishing Tree
That makes his Eaters lose the memorie
Of name and countrie. Then he brought, withall,              200
Much wood, whose sight into his serch let fall
The Art of making fire—which thus he tried:
He tooke a branch of Lawrell, amplified
Past others both in beautie and in sise,
Yet lay next hand, rubb'd it, and strait did rise            205
A warme, fume from it, Steele being that did raise
(As Agent) the attenuated Baies
To that hot vapor. So that Hermes found
Both fire first, and of it the seede close bound
In other substances; and then the seed                       210
He multiplied, of sere-wood making feed
The apt heat of it, in a pile Combin'de
Laid in a lowe Pit, that in flames strait shin'de,
And cast a sparkling crack up to the Skye,
All the drie parts so fervent were, and hye                  215
In their combustion. And how long the force
Of glorious Vulcan kept the fire in course,
So long was he in dragging from their stall
Two of the crook-hancht Herd, that ror'd withall,
And rag'd for feare t'approch the sacred fire,               220
To which did all his dreadfull powrs aspire.
When (blustring forth their breath) he on the soile
Cast both at length, though with a world of toile,
For long he was in getting them to ground
After their through-thrust and most mortall wound.           225
But worke to worke he join'd, the flesh and cut

Coverd with fat, and (on treene broches put)
In peeces rosted. But in th'Intestines
The black blood, and the honorarie chines,
Together with the carcases, lay there                    230
Cast on the cold earth, as no Deities' chere.
The Hydes upon a rugged rock he spred.
And thus were these now all in peeces shred,
And undistinguisht from Earth's common herd,
Though borne for long date and to heaven endeard,        235
And now must ever live in dead event.
But Hermes, herehence having his content,
Car'd for no more, but drew to places even
The fat-works, that, of force, must have for heaven
Their capitall ends, though stolne; and therefore were   240
In twelve parts cut, for twelve choice Deities' chere,
By this devotion. To all which he gave
Their severall honors, and did wish to have
His equall part thereof, as free and well
As th'other Deities; but the fattie smell                245
Afflicted him, though he immortall were,
Play'ng mortall parts, and being like mortalls here.
Yet his proud minde nothing the more obayde
For being a God himselfe, and his owne aide
Having to cause his due, and though in heart             250
Hee highly wisht it; but the weaker part
Subdu'd the stronger and went on in ill.
Even heavenly Powre had rather have his Will
Than have his Right; and will's the worst of All,
When but in least sort it is criminall,                  255
One Taint being Author of a Number still.
And thus (resolv'd to leave his hallow'd Hill)
First, both the fat parts and the fleshie All
Taking away, at the steepe-entryed stall

He laid all, all the feet and heads entire,                              260
And all the sere-wood, making cleare with fire.
And now, he leaving there then all things done ⎞
And finisht in their fit perfection                           ⎬
(The Coles put out, and their black Ashes throwne ⎠
From all discoverie by the lovely light                              265
The cherefull Moone cast, shyning all the Night)
He strait assum'd a novell voice's note,
And in the whirle-pit-eating flood aflote
He set his sandalls. When now, once againe
The that-morne-borne Cyllenius did attaine                              270
His Home's divine height; all the farr-stretcht waie
No one blest God encountring his assaie,
Nor Mortall Man; nor any Dogg durst spend
His borne-to-barke mouth at him; till in th'end
He reacht his Cave, and at the Gate went in                              275
Crooked, and wrapt into a fold so thin,
That no eye could discover his repayre
But as a darkness of th'Autumnall ayre.
When, going on fore-right, he strait arriv'd
At his rich Phane, his soft feet quite depriv'd                              280
Of all least noise of one that trod the earth,
They trod so swift to reach his roome of Birth.
Where in his swath-bands he his shoulders wrapt,
And (like an Infant, newly having scap't
The teeming streights) as in the Palms he lay                              285
Of his lov'd Nurse. Yet instantly would play
(Freeing his right hand) with his bearing cloth
About his knees wrapt, and strait (loosing both
His right and left hand) with his left he caught
His most-lov'd Lute. His Mother yet was taught                              290
His wanton wiles, nor could a God's wit lie
Hid from a Goddesse, who did therefore trye

[91]

His answer thus: "Why, thou made all of sleight, ⎫
And whence ariv'st thou in this rest of Night? ⎬
Improvident Impudent! In my conceipt ⎭     295
Thou rather shouldst be getting forth thy Gate,
With all flight fit for thy endanger'd State
(In merit of th'Inevitable bands
To be impos'd by vext Latona's hands,
Justly incenst for her Apollo's harms)     300
Than ly thus wrapt, as ready for her arms,
To take thee up and kisse thee. Would to heaven
(In crosse of that high grace) Thou hadst beene given
Up to Perdition, ere poore mortalls beare ⎫
Those blacke banes that thy father Thunderer ⎬     305
Hath planted thee of purpose to confer ⎭
On them and Deities!" He return'd replie:
"As Master of the feates of Policie,
Mother, why ayme you thus amisse at me,
As if I were a Sonne that Infancie     310
Could keepe from all the skill that Age can teach,
Or had in cheating but a childish reach,
And of a Mother's mandats fear'd the breach?
I mount that Art at first, that will be best
When all times consummate their cunningest,     315
Able to counsaile now my selfe and thee
In all things best, to all Eternitie.
We cannot live like Gods here without gifts,
No, nor without corruption and shifts,
And, much lesse, without eating—as we must     320
In keeping thy rules and in being Just,
Of which we cannot undergoe the lodes. ⎫
Tis better here to Imitate the Gods, ⎬
And wine or wench out all time's Periods, ⎭
To that end growing rich in readie heapes,     325

A Hymne to Hermes

Stor'de with Revennews, being in corne-fielde reapes
Of infinite Acres, than to live enclos'd
In Caves, to all Earth's sweetest ayre expos'd.
I as much honor hold as Phœbus does;
And if my Father please not to dispose                    330
Possessions to me, I my selfe will see
If I can force them in, for I can be
Prince of all Theeves. And if Latona's Sonne
Make after my stealth Indignation,
I'le have a Scape as well as he a Serch,                   335
And overtake him with a greater lurch—
For I can post to Pythos, and breake through
His huge house there, where harbors wealth enough,
Most precious Tripods, Caldrons, Steele, and Gold,
Garments rich wrought, and full of liberall fold,         340
All which will I at pleasure owne, and thow
Shalt see all, wilt thou but thy sight bestow."
    Thus chang'd great words the Gote-hyde-wearer's
        Sonne,
And Maia of Majestique fashion.
    And now the Ayre-begot Aurora rose                     345
From out the Ocean great-in-ebbs-and-flows,
When, at the never-shorne, pure-and-faire Grove
Onchestus, consecrated to the love
Of round-and-long-neckt Neptune, Phœbus found
A man whom heavie yeares had prest halfe round,           350
And yet at worke in plashing of a Fence
About a Vineyeard, that had residence
Hard by the high-way; whom Latona's Sonne
Made it not strange, but first did question
And first saluted: "Ho! you! Aged syre                     355
That here are hewing from the Vine the Bryre,
For certaine Oxen I come here t'enquire

[93]

Out of Pieria; femalls All, and rer'd
All with hornes wreath'd, unlike the common Herde;
A Cole-black Bull fed by them all alone;                                    360
And all observ'd for preservation
Through all their foodie and delicious Fen
With foure fierce Mastifs, like one-minded men.
These left their Doggs and Bull (which I admire)
And when was nere set Daie's eternall fire,                                 365
From their fierce Guardians, from their delicate fare,
Made clere departure. To me then declare,
O ould man, long since borne, if thy grave raie
Hath any man seene making stealthfull waie
With all those Oxen." Th'Olde man made replie: ⎫                            370
"Tis hard, O friend, to render readily            ⎬
Account of all that may invade mine eye,          ⎭
For many a Travailer this high-way tredds,
Some in much ill's serch, some in noble thredds
Leading their lives out; but I this young Day,                             375
Even from her first point, have made good display
Of all men passing this abundant hill
Planted with Vines, and no such stealthfull ill
Her light hath showne me. But last Evening late
I sawe a Thing that shew'd of childish state                               380
To my ould lights, and seem'd as he pursude
A Herd of Oxen with brave Heads indude—
Yet but an Infant, and retainde a Rodd,
Who warilie both this and that way trodd,
His head still backwards turn'd." This th'ould
      Man spake;                                                           385
Which he well thought upon, and swiftly brake
Into his Pursuit with abundant wing,
That strooke but one plaine ere he' knew the thing
That was the Theefe to be th'Impostor borne,

Whom Jove yet with his Sonne's name did adorne.    390
In studie and with Ardor then the King,
Jove's dazeling Sonne, plac't his exploring wing
On sacred Pylos for his forced Heard,
His ample shoulders in a cloud ensphear'd
Of fierie chrimsine. Strait the steps he found    395
Of his stolne Herd, and said: "Strange sights confound
My apprehensive powers, for here I see
The Tracts of Oxen, but aversivelie
Converted towards the Pierian Hills,
As Tredding to their Meade of Daffodills;    400
But nor mine eye Men's feet nor Women's drawes,
Nor hoarie Wolves', nor Beares', nor Lyons' Paws,
Nor thick-neckt Bulls' they show. But hee that does
These monstrous Deeds, with never so swift shooes
Hath past from that howre hither, but from hence    405
His foule course may meete fouler consequence."
With this tooke Phœbus wing, and Hermes still
(For all his Threats) secure lay in his Hill
Wall'd with a woodd; and more, a Rock, beside,
Where a Retreat rann, deepely multiplied    410
In blinding shadows, and where th'endlesse Bride
Bore to Saturnius his Ingenious Sonne—
An Odor, worth a Heart's desire, being throwne
Along the Heaven-sweet Hill, on whose Herb fedd
Rich flocks of sheepe, that bow not where they tredd    415
Their horney Pasterns. There the light of Men,
Jove's Sonne Apollo, strait descended then
The Marble Pavement in that gloomie Den.
On whom when Jove and Maia's Sonne set eye,
Wroth for his Oxen, on then instantly    420
His Odorous swath-bands flew; in which as close
Th'Impostor lay, as in the coole repose

Of cast-on Ashes Harths of burning Coles
Ly in the woods hidd, under the Controules
Of skilfull Colyers: even so close did lie                    425
Inscrutable Hermes in Apollo's eye,
Contracting his great God-head to a small
And Infant likenesse, feet, hands, head and All.
And as a Hunter hath beene often viewd,
From Chace retir'd, with both his hands embrewd     430
In his Game's blood, that doth for water call
To clense his hands, and to provoke withall
Delightsome sleepe, new washt and laid to rest;
So now lay Hermes in the close comprest
Chace of his Oxen, his New-found-out Lute           435
Beneath his arme held, as if no pursuite
But that Prise, and the virtue of his play,
His heart affected. But to Phœbus lay
His close Heart open; and he likewise knew
The brave Hyll-Nymph there and her deare Sonne, new-    440
Borne, and as well wrapt in his wiles as weeds.
All the close shrouds, too, for his Rapinous deedes
In All the Cave he knew; and with his key
He open'd three of them, in which there lay
Silver and Gold-heapes, Nectar infinite store,       445
And Deare Ambrosia; and of weedes she wore
(Pure white, and Purple) a rich Wardrobe shin'de,
Fit for the blest States of powrs so divin'de.
All which discoverd, thus to Mercurie
He offerd Conference: "Infant! you that lie          450
Wrapt so in swath-bands, instantly unfold
In what conceald Retreats of yours you hold
My Oxen stolne by you; or strait we shall
Jarr, as beseemes not powrs Celestiall.
For I will take and hurle Thee to the Deepes         455

Of dismall Tartarus, where ill Death keepes
His gloomie and inextricable fates,
And to no Eye that light Illuminates
Mother nor Father shall returne thee free,
But under Earth shall Sorrow fetter thee,                    460
And few repute thee their Superiour."
   On him replied Craft's subtlest Counsailor:
"What cruell speech hath past Latona's Care!
Seekes he his stolne-wilde-Cows where Deities are?
I have nor seene nor heard, nor can report            465
From others' mouthes one word of their resort
To any stranger. Nor will I, to gaine
A base Reward, a false Relation faine.
Nor would I, could I tell. Resemble I
An Ox-Theefe, or a Man? Especiallie                    470
A man of such a courage, such a force
As to that labour goes, that violent course?
No Infant's worke is That. My powres aspire
To sleepe and quenching of my hunger's fire
With Mother's Milke, and gainst cold shades to arme      475
With Cradle-cloths my shoulders, and Baths warme,
That no man may conceive the warr you threat
Can spring in cause from my so peacefull heat.
And even amongst th'Immortalls it would beare
Event of absolute Miracle, to heare                    480
A new-borne Infant's forces should transcend
The limits of his Dores, much lesse contend
With untam'd Oxen. This speech nothing seemes
To savour the Decorum of the Beames
Cast round about the Ayre Apollo breakes,              485
Where his divine minde her intention speakes.
I brake but yesterday the blessed wombe;
My feet are tender, and the common Tombe

[97]

Of men (the Earth) lies sharpe beneath their tred.
But, if you please, even by my Father's head                     490
I'le take the great Oath, that nor I protest
My selfe to Author on your Interest
Any such usurpation, nor have I
Seene any other that felloniously
Hath forc't your Oxen. Strange thing! What are those             495
Oxen of yours? Or what are Oxen? Knowes
My rude minde, thinke you? My eares onely touch
At their renowne, and heare that there are such."

    This speech he past; and ever as he spake
Beames from the hayre about his eye-lidds brake,                 500
His eye-brows up and downe cast, and his eye
Every way look't askans and careleslie,
And he into a loftie whistling fell,
As if he idle thought Apollo's spell.

    Apollo (gently smiling) made Replie:                      505
"O thou Impostor! whose thoughts ever lye
In labour with Deceipt! For certaine, I
Retaine Opinon that thou (even thus soone)
Hast ransackt many a House, and not in one
Night's-worke alone, nor in one Countrie neither,               510
Hast beene beseeging House and Man together,
Rigging and rifeling all waies, and no Noise
Made with thy soft feete, where it all destroies.
Soft, therefore, well, and tender thou maist call
The feet that thy stealths goe and fly withall;                 515
For many a field-bredd Herdsman (unheard still)
Hast thou made drowne the Caverns of the Hill
Where his Retreates lie with his helplesse teares,
When any flesh-stealth thy desire endeares,
And thou encountrest either flocks of sheepe                    520
Or Herds of Oxen! Up then! doe not sleepe

Thy last Nap in thy Cradle, but come downe
(Companion of black Night) and for this Crowne
Of thy young Rapines beare (from all) the state
And stile of Prince Theefe into endlesse Date."     525
    This said, he tooke the Infant in his Armes,
And with him the remembrance of his harmes,
This Præsage utt'ring, lifting him aloft:
"Be ever more the miserablie-soft
Slave of the bellie, Pursuivant of all,     530
And Author of all mischiefs Capitall."
    He scorn'd his Prophesie so he Nees'd in's face
Most forciblie, which hearing, his embrace
He loth'd, and hurl'd him gainst the ground; yet still
Tooke seate before him; though (with all the ill     535
He bore by him) he would have left full faine
That Hewer of his heart so into twaine.
Yet salv'd all thus: "Come, you so swadl'd thing!
Issue of Maia and the Thunder's King,
Be confident I shall hereafter finde     540
My brode-browd Oxen, my Prophetique minde
So farr from blaming this thy course that I
Foresee thee in it to Posteritie
The guide of All Men, All waies, to their ends."
    This spoken, Hermes from the Earth Ascends,     545
Starting Aloft, and as in Studie went,
Wrapping himselfe in his Integument;
And thus askt Phœbus: "Whither force you Me,
Farr-shot and farr most powrefull Deitie?
I know (for all your fayning) y'are still wroth     550
About your Oxen, and suspect my Troth.
O Jupiter! I wish the generall Race
Of all Earth's Oxen rooted from her face.
I steale your Oxen? I againe professe

That neither I have stolne them, nor can ghesse          555
Who else should steale them. What strange Beasts are these
Your so-lov'd Oxen? I must say (to please
Your humor thus farr) that even My few Hoowres
Have heard their fame. But be the sentence yours
Of the Debate betwixt us, or to Jove          560
(For more indifferencie) the Cause remove."
     Thus when the Solitude-affecting God
And the Latonian seede had laid abroad
All things betwixt them, (though not yet agreed,
Yet might I speake) Apollo did proceede,          565
Nothing unjustly, to charge Mercurie
With stealing of the Cows he does denie.
But his Profession was, with filed speach
And Craft's faire Complements, to overreach
All, and even Phœbus. Who because he knew          570
His Trade of subtletie, he still at view
Hunted his Foe through all the sandie waie
Up to Olympus—nor would let him straie
From out his sight, but kept behinde him still.
     And now they reacht the Odoriferous Hill          575
Of high Olympus, to their Father Jove,
To Arbitrate the Cause in which they strove.
Where, before both, Talents of justice were
Propos'd for him whom Jove should sentence Clere
In cause of their contention. And now          580
About Olympus (ever-crown'de with snow)
The rumor of their controversie flew.
All the Incorruptible, to their view,
On heaven's steepe Mountaine made return'd repaire.
     Hermes and He that light hurls through the ayre          585
Before the Thunderer's knees stood; who begunn
To question thus farr his Illustrious Sonne:

"Phœbus! To what end bringst thou Captive here
Him in whom my Minde putts delights so deare?
This New-borne Infant, that the place supplies          590
Of Herrald yet to all the Deities?
This serious busines you may witnesse drawes
The Deities' whole Court to discusse the cause."
   Phœbus replied: "And not unworthie is
The cause of all the Court of Deities.          595
For you shall heare it comprehends the weight
Of Devastation, and the verie height
Of spoile and rapine, even of Deities' rights.
Yet you (as if my selfe lov'd such delights)
Use words that wound my heart. I bring you here          600
An Infant that, even now, admits no Pere
In rapes and robb'ries. Finding out his Place
(After my measure of an infinite space)
In the Cyllenian Mountaine, such a one
In all the Art of opprobration          605
As not in all the Deities I have seene,
Nor in th'Oblivion-marckt whole Race of men.
In Night he drave my Oxen from their Leas,
Along the loftie rore-resounding Seas,
From out the Rode way quite; the steps of them          610
So quite transpos'd as would amaze the beame
Of any minde's eye, being so infinite much
Involv'd in doubt as showd a Deified touch
Went to the work's performance—all the way
Through which my cross-hov'd Cows hee did convaie          615
Had dust so darklie-hard to serch, and He
So past all measure-wrapt in subtiltie:
For nor with feet nor hands he form'd his steps
In passing through the drie waie's sandie heaps,
But us'd another counsaile to keepe hidd          620

[101]

His monstrous Tracts, that showd as one had slid
On Oke or other Boughs, that swept out still ⎫
The footsteps of his Oxen and did fill      ⎬
Their prints up ever, to the Daffodill       ⎭
(Or daintie feeding Meddow) as they trodd,                    625
Driven by this cautelous and Infant God.
   "A Mortall Man yet saw him driving on
His Prey to Pylos. Which when he had done
And got his Passe sign'd, with a sacred fire,
In peace and freely (though to his desire,                    630
Not to the Gods, he offerd part of these
My ravisht Oxen) he retires, and lies
Like to the gloomie Night in his dimm Denn,
All hid in darknesse; and in clouts againe
Wrapt him so closely that the sharpe-seene eye               635
Of your owne Eagle could not see him lye.
For with his hands the ayre he rarified
(This way and that mov'd) till bright gleames did glide
About his Being, that, if any eye             ⎫
Should dare the Darknesse, Light appos'd so nie ⎬            640
Might blinde it quite with her Antipathie—    ⎭
Which wile he wove in curious care t'illude
Th'Extreame of any eye that could intrude.
On which relying, he outrageouslie          ⎫
(When I accus'd him) trebled his replie:     ⎬              645
'I did not see, I did not heare, nor I        ⎭
Will tell at all, that any other stole
Your brode-browd Beeves. Which an Impostor's soule
Would soone have done, and any Author faine
Of purpose onely a Reward to gaine.'                          650
And thus he colourd truth in every lie."
   This said, Apollo sate; and Mercurie       ⎫
The Gods' Commander pleas'd with this replie: ⎭

"Father! I'le tell the truth (for I am true
And farr from Art to lie). He did pursue                655
Even to my Cave his Oxen this selfe daie,
The Sunn new raising his illustrious raie;
But brought with him none of the Bliss-indu'd,
Nor any ocular witnesse, to conclude
His bare assertion. But his owne command              660
Laid on with strong and necessarie hand,
To showe his Oxen, using Threats to cast
My poore and Infant powrs into the Vast
Of ghastlie Tartarus, because he beares
Of strength-sustayning youth the flaming yeares,       665
And I but yesterday produc'd to light.
By which it fell into his owne fre sight
That I in no similitude apper'd
Of powre to be the forcer of a Herde.
And credite me, O Father, since the Grace             670
Of that name in your stile you please to place,
I drave not home his Oxen, no, nor preast
Past mine owne threshold; for tis manifest
I reverence with ray soule the Sunn, and all
The knowing dwellers in this heavenly Hall,           675
Love you, observe the least; and tis most cleare
In your owne knowledge that my Merits beare
No least guilt of his blame. To all which I
Dare adde heaven's great oath, boldly swearing by
All these so well-built Entries of the Blest.          680
And therefore when I saw my selfe so prest
With his reproches, I confesse I burn'd
In my pure gall, and harsh replie return'd.
Adde your aid to your Yonger then, and free
The scruple fixt in Phœbus' Jelousie."                685
    This said, he winckt upon his Sire, and still

His swath-bands held beneath his arme—no Will
Discernd in him to hide, but have them showne.
   Jove laught aloud at his Ingenious Sonne,
Quitting himselfe with Art, so likely wrought      690
As showd in his heart not a rapinous thought;
Commanding Both to beare attorned mindes
And seeke out th'Oxen; in which serch he bindes
Hermes to play the Guide, and show the Sunn
(All grudge exilde) the Shrowd to which he wunn      695
His fayre-eyd Oxen. Then his forehead bow'd
For signe it must be so, and Hermes show'd
His free obedience. So soone he enclin'd
To his perswasion and command his minde.
   Now, then, Jove's Jarring Sonnes no longer stood,      700
But sandie Pylos and th'Alphæan flood
Reacht instantly, and made as quick a fall
On those rich-feeding fields and loftie stall
Where Phœbus' Oxen Hermes safelie kept,
Driven in by night. When sodainely he stept      705
Up to the stonie Cave, and into light
Drave forth the Oxen. Phœbus at first sight
Knew them the same, and saw apart dispread
Upon a high-rais'd rock the hydes new flead
Of th'Oxen sacrifis'd. Then Phœbus said:      710
"O thou in craftie counsailes undisplaid!
How couldst thou cut the throtes and cast to Earth
Two such huge Oxen, being so young a birth
And a mere Infant? I admire thy force
And will, behinde thy back. But this swift course      715
Of growing into strength, thou hadst not need
Continue any long Date, O thou seed
Of honor'd Maia!" Hermes (to shew how
He did those Deedes) did forthwith cut and bow

Strong Osiers in soft folds, and strappl'd strait          720
One of his hugest Oxen, all his weight
Lay'ng prostrate on the earth at Phœbus' feet,
All his foure cloven hoves easly made to greete
Each other upwards, all together brought.
In all which bands yet all the Beast's powres wrought      725
To rise and stand; when all the Herd about
The mighty Hermes rusht in, to help out
Their fellow from his fetters. Phœbus' view    ⎱
Of all this up to Admiration drew              ⎰
Even his high forces. And sterne lookes he threw ⎭          730
At Hermes for his Herd's wrong and the place
To which he had retir'd them, being in grace
And fruitfull riches of it so entire;
All which set all his force on envious fire,
All whose heat flew out of his eyes in flames,             735
Which faine he would have hidd, to hide the shames
Of his ill govern'd passions. But with ease
Hermes could calme them, and his humors please
Still at his pleasure, were he ne're so great
In force and fortitude, and high in heat.                  740
In all which he his Lute tooke, and assaid
A Song upon him, and so strangely plaid
That from his hand a ravishing horror flew—
Which Phœbus into laughter turn'd, and grew
Pleasant past measure; Tunes so artfull clere              745
Strooke even his heart-strings, and his minde made heare.
His Lute so powerfull was in forcing love
(As his hand rul'd it) that from him it drove
All feare of Phœbus; yet he gave him still
The upper hand; and (to advance his skill)                 750
To utmost Miracle he plaid sometimes
Single awhile; in which, when all the Clymes

Of rapture he had reacht (to make the Sunn
Admire enough) O then his voice would runn
Such points upon his play, and did so move,       755
They tooke Apollo Prisoner to his love.
And now the deathlesse Gods and deathfull Earth
He sung, beginning at their either's Birth
To full extent of all their Emperie.
And, first, the honor to Mnemosyne,       760
The Muses' Mother, of all Goddesse states
He gave, even forc't too't by the equall fates.
And then (as it did in Prioritie fall
Of Age and Birth) He celebrated All.
And with such Elegance and Order sung       765
(His Lute still toucht, to stick more off his tongue)
That Phœbus' heart with infinite love he eate.
Who, therefore, thus did his Deserts entreate:
   "Master of Sacrifice! chiefe soule of feast!
Patient of all paines! Artizan so blest       770
That all things thou canst doe in any One!
Worth fiftie Oxen is th'Invention
Of this one Lute. We both shall now, I hope,
In firme peace worke to all our wishes' scope.
Informe me (thou that every way canst winde,       775
And turne to Act, all wishes of thy minde)
Together with thy birth came all thy skill?
Or did some God, or God-like man, instill
This heavenly song to thee? Me thinks I heare
A new voice, such as never yet came nere       780
The brest of any, either Man or God,
Till in thee it had Prime and Period.
What Art, what Muse that medcine can produce ⎫
For cares most curelesse, what inveterate use  ⎬
Or practise of a virtue so profuse    ⎭   785

(Which three doe all the contribution keepe
That Joy or Love conferrs, or pleasing Sleepe)
Taught thee the soveraigne facture of them all?
I of the Muses am the capitall
Consort or follower; and to these belong                    790
The grace of dance, all worthie waies of song
And ever-florishing verse, the delicate Set
And sound of Instruments. But never yet
Did anything so much affect my minde
With joy and care to compasse as this kinde               795
Of Song and Play, that for the spritely feast
Of florishing assemblies are the best
And aptest works that ever Worth gave Act.
My powres with admiration stand distract
To heare with what a hand to make in love                 800
Thou rul'st thy Lute. And (though thy yongst
     howres move
At full art in ould counsailes) here I vow
(Even by this Cornell Dart I use to throw)
To thee, and to thy Mother, I'le make thee
Amongst the Gods of glorious degree,                      805
Guide of Men's waies and Theirs; and will impart
To thee the mightie Imperatorie Art,
Bestowe rich gifts on thee, and in the end
Never deceive thee." Hermes (as a friend
That wrought on all advantage, and made gaine             810
His Capitall object) thus did entertaine
Phœbus Apollo: "Doe thy Dignities,
Farr-working God and circularlie wise,
Demand my vertues? Without envie I
Will, teach thee to ascend my facultie.                   815
And this Day thou shalt reach it—finding me
In Acts and Counsailes all waies kinde to thee,

As one that all things knows, and first tak'st seat
Amongst th'Immortalls, being good, and great,
And therefore to Jove's love mak'st free accesse,      820
Even out of his accomplisht Holinesse.
Great gifts he likewise gives thee; who, fame saies.
Hast wunn thy greatnesse by his will, his waies.
By him know'st all the powers Propheticall,
O thou farr-worker, and the fates of all.      825
Yea, and I know thee rich, yet apt to learne,
And even thy Wish dost but discerne and earne.
And since thy soule so burns to know the way
To play and sing as I doe, sing and play—
Play, and perfection in thy play employ;      830
And be thy care to learne things good, thy Joy.
Take thou my Lute, My Love, and give thou me
The glorie of so great a facultie.
This sweet-tun'd consort, held but in thy hand,
Sing, and perfection in thy song command.      835
For thou alreadie hast the way to speake
Fayrely and elegantly, and to breake
All eloquence into thy utterd minde.
One gift from heaven found, may another finde.
Use then securely this thy gift, and goe      840
To feasts and dances that enamour so,
And to that covetous sport of getting glory,
That Day nor Night will suffer to be sory.
Whoever does but say in verse, sings still;
Which he that can of any other skill      845
Is Capable, so he be taught by Art
And wisedome, and can speake at every part
Things pleasing to an understanding Minde;
And such a one that seekes this Lute shall finde.
Him still it teaches easely, though he plaies      850

# A Hymne to Hermes

Soft voluntaries onely, and assaies
As wanton as the sports of children are,
And (even when he aspires to singular
In all the Mast'ries he shall play or sing)
Findes the whole worke but an unhappie thing,        855
He, I say, sure shall of this Lute be King.
But he, whoever rudely sets upon
Of this Lute's skill th'Inquest of Question
Never so ardently and angrilie,
Without the aptnesse and habilitie        860
Of Art and Nature fitting, never shall
Aspire to this, but utter triviall
And idle accents, though sung ne're so lowd,
And never so commended of the Crowde.
But thee I know, O Eminent Sonne of Jove,        865
The fiery Learner of what ever Love
Hath sharpn'd thy affections to achive.
And thee I give this Lute. Let us now live
Feeding upon the Hill-and-horse-fed Earth
Our never-handled Oxen; whose deare Birth        870
(Their femalls fellowd with their Males) let flowe
In store enough hereafter; nor must you
(However cunning-hearted your wits are)
Boile in your Gall a Grudge too circulare."
    Thus gave he him his Lute, which he embrac't,        875
And gave againe a Gode, whose bright head cast
Beames like the light forth; leaving to his care
His Oxen's keeping—which, with joyfull fare,
He tooke on him. The Lute Apollo tooke
Into his left hand, and aloft he shooke        880
Delightsome sounds up, to which God did sing.
    Then were the Oxen to their endlesse Spring
Turn'd; and Jove's Two illustr'ous Off-springs flew

Up to Olympus, where it ever snew,
Delighted with their Lute's sound all the way—      885
Whom Jove much joi'd to see, and endlesse stay
Gave to their knot of friendship. From which date
Hermes gave Phœbus an eternall state
In his affection, whose sure pledge and signe
His Lute was, and the Doctrine so divine      890
Jointly conferd on him—which well might be
True Symbole of his Love's simplicitie.
    On th'other part, Apollo in his friend
Form'd th'Art of Wisedome, to the binding end
Of his vow'd friendship; and (for further meede)      895
Gave him the farr-heard fistularie Reede.
    For all these forms of friendship, Phœbus yet
Feard that both forme and substance were not mett
In Mercurie's intentions; and, in plaine,
Said (since he saw him borne to craft and gaine,      900
And that Jove's will had him the honor done
To change at his will the possession
Of others' Goods) he fear'd his breach of vowes
In stealing both his Lute and curving Bowes,
And therefore wisht that what the Gods affect      905
Himselfe would witnesse, and to his request
His head Bow, swearing by th'Impetuous flood
Of Styx that of his whole possessions not a Good
He would diminish, but therein maintaine
The full content in which his Minde did raigne.      910
And then did Maia's Sonne his fore-head bow,
Making, by all that he desir'd, his vow
Never to prey more upon any Thing
In just possession of the farr-shot King,
Nor ever to come neare a House of his.      915
    Latonian Phœbus bowd his Brow to this

# A Hymne to Hermes

With his like promise, say'ng: "Not any One
Of all the Gods, nor any Man, that Sonne
Is to Saturnius is more deare to me,
More trusted, nor more honord, is than thee—  920
Which, yet with greater Gifts of Deitie
In future I'le confirme, and give thy state
A Rodd that riches shall accumulate,
Nor leave the bearer thrall to Death, or fate,
Or any sicknesse. All of Gold it is,  925
Three-leav'd, and full of all felicities.
And this shall be thy Guardian; this shall give
The Gods to thee in all the truth they live.
And finally, shall this the Tutresse be
Of all the words and workes informing me  930
From Jove's high counsailes, making knowne to thee
All my instructions. But to Prophesie,
O best of Jove's belov'd, and that high skill
Which to obtaine lies burning in thy will,
Nor thee, nor any God, will Fate let learne.  935
Onely Jove's minde hath insight to discerne
What that importeth; yet am I allowd
(My knowne faith trusted, and my forhead bowd,
Our great Oath taken, to resolve to none
Of all th'Immortalls the restriction  940
Of that deepe knowledge) of it All the Minde.
Since then it sits in such fast bounds confinde,
O Brother, when the Golden rodd is held
In thy strong hand, seeke not to have reveal'd
Any sure fate that Jove will have conceald—  945
For no man shall, by know'ng, prevent his fate.
And therefore will I hold in my free state
The powre to hurt and helpe what man I will,
Of all the greatest, or least toucht with ill,

That walke within the Circle of mine eye,                    950
In all the Tribes and Sexes it shall trye.
   "Yet, truely, any man shall have his will
To reape the fruites of my Prophetique skill,
Whoever seekes it by the voice or wing
Of Birds, borne truely such events to sing.                  955
Nor will I falsly, nor with fallacies,
Infringe the truth on which his faith relies;
But he that Truths in chattering plumes would finde
(Quite opposite to them that prompt my Minde)
And learne by naturall forgers of vaine lyes                 960
The more-than-ever-certaine Deities,
That man shall Sea-waies tred that leave no Tracts,
And false or no guide finde for all his facts.
And yet will I his Gifts accept as well
As his to whom the simple Truth I tell.                      965
   "One other thing to thee I'le yet make knowne,
Maia's exceedingly renowned sonne
And Jove's, and of the Gods' whole session
The most ingenious Genius. There dwell
Within a crooked Crannie, in a Dell                          970
Beneath Parnassus, certaine sisters borne,
Call'd Parcæ, whom extreame swift wings adorne,
Their Number three, that have upon their heads
White Barly floure still sprinckled, and are maids;
And these are schoole-Mistresses of things to come,         975
Without the gift of Prophecie; of whom
(Being but a boy, and keeping Oxen nere)
I learn'd their skill, though my great Father were
Careless of it, or them. These flying from home
To others' roofes, and fedd with Hony-come,                 980
Command all skill, and (being enraged then)
Will freely tell the Truths of things to Men.

[112]

But if they give them not that Gods' sweete meat,
They then are apt to utter their deceit,
And leade Men from their way. And these will I          985
Give thee hereafter, when their scrutinie
And truth thou hast both made and learn'd; and then
Please thy selfe with them, and the Race of men
(Wilt thou know any) with thy skill endeare— ⎫
Who will (be sure) afford it greedie eare, ⎬          990
And heare it often if it, prove sincere. ⎭
    "Take these, O Maia's Sonne, and in thy care
Be Horse and Oxen, all such Men as are
Patient of labour, Lyons, white-tooth'd Bores,
Mastifs, and flocks that feede the flowrie shores,          995
And every foure-foot Beast—all which shall stand
In awe of thy high Imperatory hand.
Be thou to Dis, too, sole Ambassador,
Who (though all gifts and bounties he abhor)
On thee he will bestowe a wealthie One."          1000
    Thus King Apollo honor'd Maia's Sonne
With all the rights of friendship—all whose love
Had Imposition from the Will of Jove.
    And thus with Gods and Mortalls Hermes liv'd,
Who truely helpt but few, but all deceiv'd          1005
With an undifferencing respect, and made
Vaine words and false perswasions his Trade.
His Deeds were all associats of the Night,
In which his close wrongs car'd for no man's Right.
    So all salutes to Hermes that are due,          1010
Of whom, and all Gods, shall my Muse sing true.

THE END OF THE HYMNE TO HERMES

## *A HYMNE TO VENUS*

The force, O Muse, and functions now unfold
Of Cyprian Venus, grac't with Mines of Gold,
Who even in Deities lights Love's sweet desire,
And all Death's kindes of men makes kisse her fire,
All Ayre's wing'd Nation, all the Belluine                   5
That or the Earth feedes or the Seas confine—
To all which appertaine the love and care
Of well-crown'd Venus' works. Yet three there are
Whose mindes she neither can deceive nor move—
Pallas, the seede of Ægis-bearing Jove,                     10
Who still lives Indevirginate, her eyes
Being blew and sparkling like the freezing skies,
Whom all the Gold of Venus never can
Tempt to affect her facts with God or Man.
She loving strife, and Mars his working Banes,             15
Pitcht fields and fights, and famous Artizanes,
Taught earthie men first all the Arts that are,      ⎫
Charriots, and all the frames vehiculare,            ⎬
Chiefely with brasse arm'd and adorn'd for warre—   ⎭
Where Venus onely soft-skinnd wenches fills                20
With wanton House-Works, and suggests those skills
Still to their studies. Whom Diana neither,
That beares the Golden distaft, and together
Calls Horns and Hollows, and the cries of Houndes,
And ownes the Epithete of loving sounds                    25
For their sakes, springing from such spritely sports,
Can catch with her kinde Lures—but hill resorts
To wilde-Beasts' slaughters, accents farr-off heard
Of Harps and Dances, and of woods unsheard
The sacred shades she loves, yet likes as well             30
Citties where good men and their off-spring dwell.

The third whom her kinde Passions nothing please
Is Virgine Vesta, whom Saturnides
Made reverend with his counsailes, when his Sire
That advers counsailes agitates life's fire      35
Had kindled in her, being his last begot—
Whom Neptune wow'd to knit with him the knot
Of honord Nuptialls, and Apollo too;
Which, with much vehemence she refus'd to doe,
And sterne Repulses put upon them both,      40
Adding to all her vows the Gods' great Oath,
And touching Jove's chynn (which must consummate
All vows so bound) that she would hold her state,
And be th'Invincible Maid of Deities
Through all her daies' dates. For Saturnides      45
Gave her a faire gift in her Nuptialls' stedd,
To sit in midst of his house and be fedd
With all the free and richest feast of Heaven,
In all the Temples of the Gods being given
The prise of honor. Not a mortall Man      50
(That either, of the powrs Olympian
His half-birth having, may be said to be ⎫
A mortall of the Gods, or else that he ⎬
[Deities' wills doings] is of Deitie) ⎭
But gives her honor of the amplest kinde.      55
Of all these Three can Venus not a Minde
Deceive, or set on forces to reflect.
Of all powrs els yet not a sex nor sect
Flies Venus—either of the blessed Gods,
Or Men confin'de in mortall Periods.      60
But even the Minde of Jove she doth seduce,
That chides with Thunder so her lawlesse use
In humane Creatures, and by lot is given
Of all most honor, both in Earth and Heaven.

And yet even his all-wise and mightie Minde          65
She, when she lists, can forge affectes to blinde,
And mixe with mortall Dames his Deitie,
Conceald at all parts from the jelous eye
Of Juno, who was both his sister borne
And made his wife, whom beautie did adorne          70
Past all the Bevie of immortall Dames,
And whose so chiefely-glorified Flames
Crosse-counsailde Saturne got, and Rhea bore, ⎱
And Jove's pure counsailes (being Conqueror)  ⎬
His wife made of his sister—I, and more,      ⎭      75
Cast such an amorous fire into her minde
As made her (like him) with the Mortall kinde
Meete in unmeete bedd; using utmost haste,
Lest she should know that he liv'd so unchaste,
Before her selfe felt that fault in her heart,      80
And gave her tongue too just edge of Desert
To tax his lightnes. With this End, beside,
Lest laughter-studying Venus should deride
The Gods more than the Goddesses, and say
That shee the Gods commixt in amorous play          85
With mortall Dames, begetting mortall seede
T'Immortall sires, and not make Goddesses breede
The like with mortall Fathers, but t'acquite
Both Gods and Goddesses of her despite,
Jove tooke (even in her selfe) on him her powre,    90
And made her with a mortall Paramoure
Use as deform'd a mixture as the rest;
Kindling a kinde affection in her brest
To God-like-limm'd Anchises, as he kept
On Ida's top-on-top-to-heaven's-Pole-heapt          95

[95]. Ἀκροπόλος, Altissimum habens verticem, cujus summitas ipsum polum attingit.

Amongst the manie fountaines there his Herd;
For after his brave Person had apper'de
To her bright eye, her heart flew all on fire,
And (to amaze) she burn'd in his desire,
Flew strait to Cyprus, to her odorous Phane          100
And Altars that the people Paphiane
Advanc't to her. Where (soone as entred) shee
The shyning gates shut, and the Graces three
Washt, and with Oiles of everlasting sent
Bath'd, as became her deathlesse Iyneament.          105
Then her Ambrosian Mantle she assum'd,
With rich and odoriferous Ayres perfum'd—
Which being put on, and all her Trimms beside
Fayre, and with all allurements amplified,
The All-of-Gold-made laughter-loving Dame            110
Left odorous Cyprus, and for Troy became
A swift Contendresse, her Passe cutting All
Along the cloudes, and made her instant fall
On fountfull Ida, that her Mother-Brests
Gives to the Preyfull broode of savage Beasts.       115
And through the Hill she went the readie way ⎫
T'Anchises' Oxstall, where did fawne and play ⎬
About her blessed feet Wolves grislie-gray, ⎭
Terrible Lyons, many a Mankind Beare,
And Lybberds swift, insatiate of red Deare—          120
Whose sight so pleas'd that ever as she past
Through every Beast a kindely Love she cast,
That in their Denns, obscur'd with shadowes deepe,
Made all, distinguisht in kinde Couples, sleepe.
     And now she reacht the rich Pavilion           125
Of the Heroe, in whom heavens had showne
A fayre and goodly Composition
And whom she in his Oxstall found alone,

His Oxen feeding in fat Pastures by,
He walking up and downe, sounds clere and hye          130
From his harp striking. Then before him shee
Stood like a Virgine that invinciblie
Had borne her beauties, yet alluringly
Bearing her person, lest his ravisht eye
Should chance t'affect him with a stupid feare.          135
Anchises seeing her, all his senses were
With wonder stricken, and high-taken heeds
Both of her forme, brave stature, and rich weedes.
For, for a vaile, she shin'd in an Attire
That cast a radiance past the Ray of fire.          140
Beneath which wore she, guirt to her, a Gowne
Wrought all with growing-rose-budds, reaching downe
T'her slender smalls, which buskinns did divine,
Such as taught Thetis' silver Feete to shine.
Her soft white neck rich Carquenets embrac't,          145
Bright, and with gold in all variety grac't,
That, to her brests let downe, lay there and shone
As, at her joyfull full, the rising Moone.
Her sight show'd miracles. Anchises' Heart
Love tooke into his hand, and made him part          150
With these high Salutations: "Joy, O Queene!
Whoever of the Blest thy beauties beene
That light these Entries! Or the Deitie
That Darts affecteth, or that gave the eye
Of Heaven his heat and Luster! Or that moves          155
The hearts of all with all-commanding Loves!
Or generous Themis! Or the blew-eyd Maid!
Or of the Graces any that are laid
With all the Gods in comparable skales,
And whom Fame up to Immortalitie calles!          160
Or any of the Nymphs that unshorne Groves

Or that this fayre Hill-habitation loves,
Or valleys flowing with earth's fattest Goods,
Or Fountaines pouring forth eternall floods!
Say which of all thou art, that in some place          165
Of circular prospect, for thine eyes' deare grace
I may an Altar build, and to thy Powres
Make sacred all the yeare's devoted Howres
With consecrations sweet and oppulent.
Assur'd whereof, be thy benigne Minde bent          170
To these wisht blessings of me: give me parts
Of chiefe attraction in Troyan hearts;
And after give me the refulgencie
Of most renownd, and rich Posteritie,
Long and free life, and Heaven's sweet light as long,          175
The people's blessings, and a health so strong
That no disease it let my life engage,
Till th'utmost limit of a humane Age."
   To this Jove's seede this answer gave againe:
"Anchises! happiest of the humane straine!          180
I am no Goddesse. Why, a thrall to Death,
Think'st thou like those that immortality breath!
A woman brought me forth; my Father's Name
Was Otreus (if ever his high fame
Thine eares have witnest, for he governd all          185
The Phrygian State, whose every Towne a wall
Impregnable embrac't). Your, tongue, you heare,
I speake so well that in my naturall spheare
(As I pretend) it must have taken prime.
A woman, likewise of the Troyan clime,          190
Tooke of me in her house the Nurse's care
From my deare Mother's Bosome; and thus are
My words of equall accent with your owne.
How here I come (to make the reason knowne)—

Argicides, that beares the Golden Rod,                          195
Transferd me forciblie from, my Abod
Made with the Maiden Traine of her that joies
In Golden shafts, and loves so well the noise
Of Hounds and Hunters (Heaven's pure-living powre)
Where many a Nymph and maid of mighty Dowre    200
Chast sports emploid, all circkl'd with a Crowne
Of infinite Multitude, to see so showne
Our maiden Pastimes, Yet from all the Fayre
Of this so forcefull concourse, up in Ayre
The Golden-Rodd-sustaining Argus' Guide           205
Rapt me in sight of all, and made me ride
Along the Clouds with him, enforcing me,
Through many a labour of Mortalitie,
Through many an unbuilt Region and a rude,
Where savage Beasts devour'd, Preys warme and crude,  210
And would not let my feares take one foot's tred ⎫
On her by whom are all Lives comforted;          ⎬
But said my Maiden State must grace the Bed       ⎭
Of King Anchises, and bring forth to thee
Issue as faire as of divine Degree.                215
Which said, and showing me thy moving Grace,
Away flew he up to th'Immortall Race.
And thus came I to thee, Necessitie              ⎫
With her steele stings compelling me t'applie     ⎬
To her high Powre my will. But You must I          ⎭   220
Implore by Jove, and all the reference due
To your deare Parents, who (in bearing you)
Can beare no meane saile, leade me home to them
An untoucht Maid, being brought up in th'extreme
Of much too cold simplicitie to know              225
The fiery cunnings that in Venus glow.

Show me to them then, and thy Brothers borne:
I shall appeare none that parts disadorne,
But such as well may serve a Brother's wife;
And show them now, even to my future life,             230
If such or no my Present will extend.
To Horse-Breede-vary'ng Phrygia likewise send
T'Informe my Sire and Mother of my State,
That live for me extreame disconsolate—
Who Gold enough and well-woven weedes will give—     235
All whose rich Gifts in my Amends receive.
All this perform'd, adde celebration then
Of honord Nuptialls, that by God and Men
Are held in reverence." All this while she said,
Into his bosome jointly she convaid                    240
The fires of love; when (all enamourd) He
In these terms answered: "If Mortalitie
Confine thy Fortunes, and a woman were
Mother to those attractions that appeare
In thy admir'd forme, thy great Father given          245
High Name of Otreus, and the Spie of Heaven
(Immortall Mercurie) th'enforce-full cause
That made thee lose the Prize of that applause
That modestie immaculate Virgines gives,
My wife thou shall be call'd through both our lives.  250
Nor shall the powrs of Men nor Gods withhold
My fiery resolution to enfold
Thy bosome in mine armes—which here I vow
To firme performance, past delay and Now.
Nor (should Apollo with his silver Bow                 255
Shoote me to instant death) would I forbeare
To doe a deede so full of cause so deare.
For with a Heaven-sweet woman I will ly,

Though strait I stoope the house of Dis, and die."
   This said, he tooke her hand, and she tooke way     260
With him, her bright eyes casting round—whose stay
She stuck upon a bed that was before
Made for the King, and wealthie coverings wore.
On which Beares' Hydes and bigg-voic't Lyons' lay,
Whose Preyfull lives the King had made his Prey,    265
Hunting th'Idalian Hills. This Bed when they
Had both ascended, first he tooke from her
The fierie weede that was her utmost weare,
Unbutton'd her next rosie Robe, and los'd
The Gyrdle that her slender wast enclos'd,     270
Unlac't her buskinns, all her Jewellrie
Tooke from her neck and brests, and all lay'd by
Upon a Golden-studded Chaire of State.
Th'Amaze of all which being remov'd, even Fate
And counsaile of the equall Gods gave way     275
To this, that with a Deathlesse Goddesse lay
A deathfull Man, since what his love assum'd
Not with his conscious knowledge was presum'd.
   Now when the shepherds and the Herdsmen, all,
Turnd from their flowrie Pasture to their Stall     280
With all their Oxen, fat and frolick sheepe,
Venus into Anchises cast a sleepe,
Sweet and profound; while with her owne hands now
With her rich weeds she did her selfe indow,
But so distinguisht that he clere might know     285
His happie Glories. Then (to her desire
Her heavenly Person put in Trimms entire)
Shee by the bed stood of the well-built Stall,
Advanc't her head to State Celestiall,
And in her cheekes arose the radiant hew     290
Of rich-cround Venus to apparant view.

And then she rous'd him from his rest, and said:
"Up, my Dardanides, forsake thy bed.
What pleasure, late emploid, letts Humor steepe
Thy lidds in this inexcitable sleepe?                     295
Wake, and now say if I appeare to thee
Like her that first thine eyes conceited me."
 This started him from sleepe, though deepe and deare,
And passing promptlie he enjoy'd his eare.
But when his eye saw Venus' neck and eyes,                300
Whose beauties could not beare the Counterprise
Of any other, downe his owne eyes fell,
Which pallid feare did from her view repell,
And made him with a maine respect beside
Turne his whole person from her state, and hide           305
(With his rich weede appos'd) his royall face,
These wing'd words using: "When at first thy Grace
Mine eyes gave entertainment, well I knew
Thy state was Deified; but thou told'st not true;
And therefore let me pray thee (by thy Love              310
Borne to thy Father, Ægis-bearing Jove)
That thou wilt never let me live to be  ⎫
An abject, after so divine degree    ⎬
Taken in fortune, but take ruth on me.  ⎭
For any Man that with a Goddesse lies,                   315
Of interest in immortalities,
Is never long liv'd." She replied: "Forbeare,
O happiest of Mortall Men, this feare,
And rest assur'd that (not for me, at least)
Thy least ills feare fits—no, nor for the rest           320
Of all the Blessed; for thou art their friend,
And so farr from sustaining instant end
That to thy long-enlarg'd life there shall spring
Amongst the Troyans a deare Sonne, and King,

To whom shall many a Sonne and Sonne's Sonne rise        325
In everlasting-great Posterities,
His Name Æneas—therein keeping life
For ever in my much-conceipted griefe,
That I (immortall) fell into the bed
Of one whose blood Mortality must shed.        330
But rest thou comforted, and all the Race
That Troy shall propagate in this high grace—
That past all Races else the Gods stand nere ⎫
Your glorious Nation, for the formes ye beare ⎬
And Natures so ingenuous and sincere.       ⎭        335
For which, the great in counsailes, Jupiter,
Your Gold-lockt Ganymedes did transfer
(In rapture farr from men's depressed fates)
To make him Consort with our Deified states,
And skale the Tops of the Saturnian skies,        340
He was so meere a Marveile in their eyes.
And therefore from a Bolle of Gold he fills
Redd Nectar, that the rude distension kills
Of windes that in your humane stomacks breede.
But then did Languor on the Liver feede        345
Of Tros, his Father, that was King of Troy,
And ever did his memorie employ
With losse of his deare bewtie so bereven, ⎫
Though with a sacred whirlewinde rapt to heaven. ⎬
But Jove (in pittie of him) saw him given       ⎭        350
Good compensation, sending by Heaven's Spye
White-swift-hov'd Horse, that Immortality
Had made firme spirrited; and had (beside)
Hermes to see his Ambassie supplied
With this vow'd Bountie (using all at large        355

[345]. ἄληστος, Cujus memoria erit perpetua.

[124]

That his unaltered counsailes gave in charge)
That he himselfe should Immortality breath,
Expert of Age and Woe as well as Death.
    "This Ambassie exprest, he mourn'd no more,
But up with all his inmost minde he bore,        360
Joying that he upon his swift-hov'd Horse
Should be sustain'd in an eternall course.
    "So did the golden-thron'de Aurora raise
Into her Lap another that the praise
Of an Immortall fashion had in Fame,        365
And of your Nation bore the Noble Name—
His Title Tithon, who, not pleas'd with her
As she his lovely Person did transfer,
(To satisfie him) she bad aske of Jove
The Gift of an Immortall for her Love.        370
Jove gave, and bound it with his bowed Brow,
Performing to the utmost point his vow.
Foole that she Was, that would her love engage,
And not as long aske from the Bane of Age
The sweet exemption, and Youth's endlesse flowre!        375
Of which as long as both the grace and power
His person ehtertainde, she lov'd the Man,
And (at the fluents of the Ocean
Nere Earth's extreame bounds) dwelt with him:
    but when
(According to the course of aged Men)        380
On his faire head and honorable Beard
His first gray hayres to her light eyes apperd,
She left his bed, yet gave him still for food
The Gods' Ambrosia, and attire as good—
Till even the hare of Age came on so fast        385
That not a lyneament of his was grac't
With powre of Motion, nor did still sustaine

(Much lesse) the Vigor had t'advance a vaine,
The virtue lost in each exhausted limm
That (at his wish) before would answer him;                    390
All Powrs so quite decaid that, when he spake,
His voice no perceptible accent brake:
Her counsaíle then thought best to strive no more,
But lay him in his bed and lock his Dore.
Such an Immortall would not I wish thee,                       395
T'extend all daies so to Eternitie.
But it, as now, thou couldst performe thy course
In Grace of Forme and all corporeall force
To an eternall Date, Thou then should'st beare
My Husband's worthie Name, and not a Teare                     400
Should I neede raine for thy deserts declinde,
From my All-clouded bitternesse of minde.
But now the sterne storme of relentlesse Age
Will quickly circkle thee, that waites t'engage
All Men alike, even Lothsomnesse and Bane                      405
Attending with it every humane wane,
Which even the Gods hate. Such a Penance lies
Impos'd on flesh and blood's infirmities,
Which I my selfe must taste in great degree,
And date as endlesse, for consorting thee.                     410
All the Immortalls with my opprobrie
Are full by this time; on their Hearts so lie
(Even to the sting of Feare) my cunnings us'd,
And wiving conversations infus'd
Into the bosomes of the best of them                           415
With women that the fraile and mortall stream
Doth daily ravish—all this long since done,
Which now no more but with effusion
Of teares, I must in Heaven so much as name,
I have so forfaited in this my Fame,                           420

And am impos'd paine of so great a kinde
For so much erring from a Goddesse' Minde.
For I have put beneath my Gyrdle here
A Sonne whose sire the humane mortall sphere
Gives Circumscription. But when first the light                    425
His eyes shall comfort, Nymphs that hant the height
Of Hills, and Brests have of most deepe receit,
Shall be his Nurses; who inhabit now
A Hill of so vast and divine a Brow
As Man nor God can come at their Retreates;                        430
Who live long lives, and eat immortall Meates,
And with Immortalls in the exercise
Of comely Dances dare contend, and rise
Into high Question which deserves the Prise.
The light Sileni mix in love with These,                           435
And of all Spies the Prince, Argicides,
In well-trymmd Caves their secret meetings made.
And with the lives of these doth life invade
Or odorous fare Trees, or high-forheaded Okes,
Together taking their begetting strokes,                           440
And have their lives and deaths of equall Dates,
Trees bearing lovely and Delightsome states,
Whom Earth first feedes, that Men initiates.
On her high Hills she doth their states sustaine,
And they their owne heights raise as high againe.                  445
   "Their Growghts together made, Nymphs Call
      their Groves
Vowd to th'Immortalls' services and loves—
Which men's steeles therefore touch not, but let grow.
But when wise Fates times (or their fadings know,
The faire Trees still before the faire Nymphs die,                 450
The Bark about them growne corrupt and drie,
And all their boughs (falne) yeeld to Earth her right;

And then the Nymphs' lives leave the lovely Light.
  "And these Nymphs in their Caves shall nurse
    my Son,
Whom (when in him Youth's first grace is begun)      455
The Nymphs, his Nurses, shall present to thee,
And shew thee what a Birth thou hast by Me.
And (sure as now I tell thee all these things)
When earth hath cloth'd her plants in five faire
    springs,
My selfe will make returne to this Retreate,      460
And bring that Flowre of thy enamour'd heate;
Whom when thou then seest, Joy shall fire thine eyes,
He shall so well Present the Deities.
And then into thine owne care take thy Sonne
From his calme seat to windie Ilion,      465
Where if strickt question be upon thee past,
Asking what Mother bore beneath her wast
So deare a Sonne, answer, as I afford
Fit admonition, nor forget a word:
'They say a Nymph, call'd Calucopides,      470
That is with others an inhabitresse
On this thy wood-crownd Hill, acknowledges
That she his life gave.' But if thou declare
The Secret's truth, and art so mad to dare,
(In glory of thy fortunes) to approve      475
That rich-crownd Venus mixt with thee in love,
Jove (fir'd with my aspersion so dispred)
Will with a wreakefull lightning dart thee dead.
  "All now is told thee; comprehend it All.
Be Master of thy selfe, and doe not call      480
My Name in question; but with reverence vow
To Deities' angers all the awe ye owe."
    This said, shee reacht Heaven, where ayres ever flowe.

## A Hymne to Venus

And so, O Goddesse, ever honord be
In thy so Odorous Cyprian Emperie!                    485
My Muse, affecting first thy Fame to raise,
Shall make Transcension now to others' Praise.

*THE END OF THE FIRST HYMNE TO VENUS*

## TO THE SAME

   The Reverend Rich-crownd, and Faire Queene I sing,
Venus, that owes in Fate the fortressing
Of all Maritimall Cyprus—where the force
Of gentle-breathing Zephyr sterde her Course
Along the waves of the resounding Sea,              5
While, yet unborne, in that soft fome she laie
That brought her forth; whom those faire Howrs
    that beare
The Golden-bridles joyfully stood nere,
Tooke up into their armes, and put on her
Weeds of a never corruptible weare.              10
On her immortall head a Crowne they plac't,
Elaborate, and with all the beauties grac't
That Gold could give it; of a weight so great
That, to impose and take off, it had set
Three Handles on it, made, for endlesse hold,     15
Of shyning Brasse and all adorn'd with Gold.
Her soft neck all with Carquenets was grac't,
That stoop't, and both her silver brests embrac't,
Which even the Howrs themselves weare in resort
To Deities' Dances and her Father's Court.      20
Grac't at all parts, they brought to Heaven her graces;
Whose first sight seene, all fell into embraces,
Hugg'd her white hands, saluted, wishing all
To weare her Maiden Flowre in festivall
Of sacred Hymen, and to leade her home—      25
All, to all admiration, overcome
With Cytheræa with the violet Crowne.
   So to the black-Browd-sweet-spoke All Renowne!

## To the Same

Prepare my Song, and give me, in the end,
The victory to whose Palme all contend!                    30
So shall my Muse for ever honour thee,
And (for thy sake) thy faire Posteritie.

## BACCHUS,
### or
### *The Pyrats*

 Of Dionysus (Noble Semele's Son)
I now intend to render Mention,
As on a prominent shore his person shone,
Like to a Youth whose flowre was newly blone.
Bright azure Tresses plaid about his head,    5
And on his bright brode shoulders was dispred
A purple Mantle. Strait he was descride
By certaine Manly Pyrats, that applide
Their utmost speede to prise him, being abord
A well-built Barck, about whose brode sides ror'd   10
The wine-black Tyrrhene Billows. Death as black
Brought them upon him in their future wrack.
For soone as they had purchast but his view,
Mutuall signes past them, and ashore they flew.
Tooke him, and brought him instantly aborde,   15
Soothing their Hopes to have obtain'd a Horde
Of riches with him—and a Jove-kept King
To such a Flowre must needes be naturall spring.
And therefore strait strong Fetters they must fetch,
To make him sure. But no such strength would stretch   20
To his constrain'd Powrs. Farr flew all their Bands
From any least force done his feet or hands.
But he sate casting smiles from his black eyes
At all their worst. At which Discoveries
Made by the Master, he did thus dehort   25
All his Associats: "Wretches! Of what sort
Hold ye the Person ye assaie to binde?
Nay, which of all the Powre fully-divin'de
Esteeme ye him, whose worth yeelds so much weight

That not our well-built Barck will beare his freight?          30
Or Jove himselfe he is, or he that beares
The silver Bowe, or Neptune. Nor appeares
In him the least resemblance of a Man,
But of a straine at least Olympian.
Come! Make we quick dismission of his state,          35
And on the black-soild earth exonerate
Our sinking vessell of his Deified Lode,
Nor dare the touch of an intangible God,
Lest windes outragious and of wrackfull scath,
And smoking Tempests, blowe his fiery wrath."          40
This well-spoke Master the Tall captaine gave
Hatefull and horrible language; call'd him slave,
And bad him mark the prosperous gale that blew,
And how their vessell with her maine saile flew;
Bade all take armes, and said their workes requir'de ⎱          45
The cares of Men, and not of an inspir'de             ⎬
Pure zealous Master—his firme hopes being fir'de ⎰
With this Opinion, that they should arive
In Ægypt strait, or Cyprus, or where live
Men whose brave breaths above the Northwinde blowe—          50
Yea, and perhaps beyond their Region too;
And that he made no doubt but in the end
To make his Prisoner tell him every friend
Of all his off-spring, Brothers, Wealth, and All;
Since that Prise, certaine, must some God let fall.          55
   This said, the Mast and maine-saile up he drew,
And in the maine saile's midd'st a franck Gale blew;
When all his ship tooke armes to brave their Prise.
But strait strange works apperde to all their eyes:
First, sweete wine through their swift-black Barck
   did flow,          60
Of which the Odors did a little blowe

Their fiery spirits, making th'Ayre so fine
That they in flood were there as well as wine.
A meere Immortall-making savour rose,
Which on the Ayre the Deitie did Impose.                    65
The Sea-Men see'ng All, Admiration seas'd.
Yet instantly their wonders were encreas'd,
For on the Top saile there rann, here and there,
A Vine that Grapes did in abundance beare,
And in an instant was the ship's maine Mast      ⎫         70
With an obscure-greene Ivie's armes embrac't,    ⎬
That florisht strait and were with Buries grac't; ⎭
Of which did Gyrlonds circle every brow
Of all the Pirats, and no One knew how.
Which when they sawe, they made the Master stere          75
Out to the shore; whom Bacchus made forbeare,
With showing more wonders. On the Hatches He
Apper'd a terrible Lyon, horriblie
Roring; and in the Mid-deck a Male Beare,
Made with a huge Mane; making all for feare               80
Crowd to the sterne about the Master there,
Whose Minde he still kept dantlesse and sincere,
But on the Captaine rusht and rampt, with force
So rude and sodaine that his maine recours
Was to the Maine-Sea strait; and after him               85
Leapt all his Mates, as trusting to their swimm
To fly foule Death—but so found what they fied,
Being all to Dolphinns metamorphosed.
The Master he tooke Ruth of, sav'd, and made
The blessedst Man that ever tried his Trade,            90
These few words giving him: "Be confident,
Thou God-inspired Pylot! in the Bent
Of my affection, readie to requite
Thy late-to-me-intended benefite.

I am the Roring God of spritely Wine,          95
Whom Semele (that did even Jove incline
To amorous Mixture, and was Cadmus' care)
Made issue to the Mighty Thunderar."
   And thus all Excellence of Grace to thee, ⎫
Sonne of sweete-count'nance-cary'ng Semele. ⎬   100
I must not thee forget in least Degree; ⎭
But pray thy spirit to render so my song
Sweete, and all waies in order'd furie strong.

## *TO MARS*

Mars, Most-strong, Gold-helm'd, making
    Chariots crack;
Never without a shield cast on thy back;
Minde-master, towne-guard, with darts never driven;
Strong-handed, All armes, fort and fence of heaven;
Father of Victory with faire strokes given;        5
Joint surrogate of Justice, lest she fall
In unjust strifes a Tyrant; Generall
Onely of Just Men justly; that dost beare
Fortitud's Scepter; to Heaven's fiery sphere
Giver of circulare motion, betweene        10
That and the Pleiads that still wandring bene;
Where thy still-vehemently-flaming Horse
About the third Heaven make their fiery course;
Helper of Mortalls; Heare! As thy fires give
The faire and present boldnesses, that strive        15
In Youth for Honor, being the sweete-beamd Light
That darts into their lives, from all thy Height,
The Fortitudes and Fortunes found in fight;
So would I likewise wish to have the Powre
To keepe off from my head thy bitter Howre,        20
And that false fire, cast from my soule's lowe kinde,
Stoope to the fit rule of my highest Minde,
Controuling that so eager sting of wrath
That styrrs me on still to that horrid scath
Of Warr, that God still sends to wreake his splene        25
(Even by whole Tribes) of proud injurious Men.
    But O thou ever-blessed! Give me still
Presence of minde to put in Act my will,
Varied, as fits, to all Occasion;
And to live free, unforc't, unwrought upon,        30

Beneath those Lawes of Peace that never are
Affected with Pollutions Populare
Of unjust hurt, or losse to any One;
And to beare safe the burthen undergone
Of Foes inflexive and inhumane hates,                    35
Secure from violent and harmefull Fates.


## TO DIANA


  Diana praise, Muse, that in Darts delights,
Lives still a Maid, and had nutritiall rights
With her borne-Brother, the farr-shooting Sunn—
That doth her all-of-Gold-made Chariot runn
In Chace of Game, from Meles that abounds          5
In black-browd Bull-rushes (and where her Hounds
She first uncouples, joyning there her Horse)
Through Smyrna, carried in most fiery course
To Grape-rich Claros, where (in his rich home,
And constant expectation she will come)            10
Sits Phœbus, that the silver Bowe doth beare,
To meete with Phœbe, that doth Darts transferre
As farr as He his shafts. As farr then be
Thy chaste Fame shot, O Queene of Archerie!
Sacring my song to every Deitie.                   15


## TO VENUS


  To Cyprian Venus, still my verses vow,
Who Gifts as sweete as honey doth bestow

On all Mortality; that ever smiles,
And rules a face that all foes reconciles;
Ever sustaining in her hand a Flowre                    5
That all desire keepes ever in her Powre.
   Haile then, O Queene of well-built Salamine
And all the state that Cyprus doth confine!
Informe my song with that celestiall fire
That in thy beauties kindles all desire.                10
So shall my Muse for ever honour Thee,
And any other thou commend'st to Me.


## TO PALLAS

   Pallas Minerva onely I beginne
To give my song; that makes warr's terrible Dinne,
Is Patronesse of Citties, and with Mars
Marshall'd in all the care and cure of wars,
And in everted Citties, fights and Cries—              5
But never doth her selfe set downe or rise
Before a Cittie, but at both times Shee
All injur'de people sets on foot and free.
   Give, with thy warr's force, Fortune then to Me,
And, with thy Wisedome's force, Felicity.              10


## TO JUNO

   Saturnia and her Throne of Gold I sing,
That was of Rhea the eternall spring,
And Empresse of a beautie never yet

Equall'd in height of Tincture—of the great
Saturnius (breaking Ayre in awfull Noise)                    5
The farr-fam'd wife and sister, whom in joies
Of high Olympus all the blessed Love
And Honour equall with unequall'd Jove.


## TO CERES

The Rich-hayr'd Ceres I assaie to sing;
A Goddesse in whose Grace the naturall spring
Of serious Majestie it selfe is seene;
And of the wedded, yet in grace stil green,
Proserpina, her Daughter, that displaies              5
A Beautie casting every way her Raies.
    All Honor to thee, Goddesse! Keepe this Towne,
    And take thou chiefe charge of my song's Renoune!


## TO THE MOTHER OF THE GODS

Mother of All, both Gods and Men, Commend,
O Muse, whose faire Forme did from Jove descend;
That doth with Cymball sounds delight her life,
And tremulous divisions of the Fife,
Love's dreadfull Lyons' Rores, and Wolves' hoarse Houles,   5
Sylvane Retreates, and Hills whose hollow knoules
Raise repercussive soundes about her eares.
    And so may Honour ever crowne thy yeares
    With All-else Goddesses, and ever be
    Exalted in the Muses' Harmonie!                    10

## TO LYON-HEARTED HERCULES

Alcides, (Force-fullest of all the Broode
Of Men enforc't with neede of earthie foode)
My Muse shal memorise; the son of Jove,
Whom, in faire seated Thebs (commixt in love
With great Heaven's sable-cloude-assembling state)    5
Alcmena bore to him, and who (in date
Of daies forepast) through all the Sea was sent
And Earth's inenarrable Continent,
To Acts that King Eurystheus had decreede;
Did many a Petulant and Imperious Deede    10
Himselfe, and therefore suffer'd many a Toile;
Yet now inhabites the illustrious Soile
Of white Olympus, and Delights his life
With still young Hebe, his well-anckled wife.
    Haile, King, and Sonne of Jove! Vouchsafe thou Me    15
    Virtue, and her Effect, Felicitie!

## TO ÆSCULAPIUS

With Æsculapius, the Phisition,
That cur'd all sicknesse, and was Phœbus' Sonne,
My Muse makes Entrie; to whose life gave yield
Divine Coronis in the Dotian field,
King Phlegius' Daughter, who much Joy on Men    5
Conferd in deare Ease of their yrkesome Paine—
    For which, my salutation, worthy King,
    And vowes to thee paid, ever when I sing!

## *TO CASTOR AND POLLUX*

Castor and Pollux, the Tyndarides,
Sweete Muse illustrate; that their Essences
Fetch from the high forms of Olympian Jove,
And were the faire fruits of bright Leda's Love,
Which shee produc't beneath the sacred shade          5
Of steepe Taygetus, being subdu'd and made
To serve th'Affections of the Thunderer.
   And so all Grace to you, whom all Aver
   (For skill in Horses and their Manage geven)
   To be the bravest Horsemen under Heaven!          10


## *TO MERCURIE*

Hermes I honor, the Cyllenian Spie,
King of Cyllenia and of Arcadie
With flocks abounding; and the Messenger
Of all th'Immortalls, that doth still inferre
Profites of infinite valew to their store;          5
Whom to Saturnius bashfull Maia bore,
Daughter of Atlas, and did therefore flie
Of all th'Immortalls the Societie
To that darcke Cave where, in the dead of Night,
Jove joind with her in Love's divine Delight,          10
When Golden sleepe shut Juno's jealous eye,
Whose arms had wrists as white as Ivorie,
From whom and all, both Men and Gods beside,
The faire-hayrd Nymph her scape kept undescride.
   Joy to the Jove-got then, and Maia's Care,          15
   Twixt Men and Gods the generall Messenger,
   Giver of good Grace, Gladnesse, and the Flood
   Of all that Men or Gods account their Good!

## TO PAN

Sing, Muse, this chiefe of Hermes' love-got Joies,
Goate-footed, Two-horn'd, amorous' of noise,
That through the faire-Greenes, al adorn'd with Trees,
Together goes with Nymphs, whose nimble knees
Can every Dance foot, that affect to scale     5
The most inaccessible Tops of all
Uprightest rocks, and ever use to call
On Pan, the bright-hayr'd God of Pastorall—
Who yet is leane and lovelesse, and, doth owe
By lot all loftiest Mountaines crown'd with snowe;     10
All Tops of Hills and cliffie Highnesses,
All Silvan Copses, and the Fortresses
Of Thorniest Queaches, here and there doth rove,
And sometimes (by allurement of his love)
Will wade the watrie softnesses. Sometimes     15
(In quite oppos'de Capriccios) he climes
The hardest Rocks and highest, every way
Running their Ridges. Often will convaie
Himselfe up to a watch-Towr's Top, where sheepe
Have their Observance; oft through Hills as steepe     20
His Gotes he runns upon, and never rests.
Then turns he head, and flies on savage Beasts,
Mad of their slaughters—so most sharpe an eye
Setting upon them as his Beames let flie
Through all their thickest Tapistries. And then     25
(When Hesp'rus calls to folde the flocks of Men)
From the greene Clossets of his loftiest Reedes
He rushes forth, and Joy with Song he feedes—
When (under shadow of their motions set)
He plaies a verse forth so profoundly sweet     30
As not the Bird that in the flowrie Spring

(Amidds the leaves set) makes the Thickets ring
Of her sowre sorrowes, sweetened with her song,
Runns her divisions varied so and strong.
And then the sweete-voic't Nymphs that crowne his
    mountaines         35
(Flockt round about the deepe-black-watred fountaines)
Fall in with their Contention of song,
To which the Echoes all the Hills along
Their repercussions add. Then here and there
(Plac't in the midd'st) the God the Guide doth beare    40
Of all their Dances, winding in and out,
A Lynce's Hide (besprinckled round about
With blood) cast on his shoulders. And thus He
With well-made songs maintaines th'alacritie
Of his free minde, in silken Meddows crownde    45
With Hyacynths and Saffrons, that abound
In sweete-breath'd Odors, that th'unnumber'd grasse
(Besides their sents) give as through all they passe.
And these, in all their pleasures, ever raise
The blessed Gods' and long Olympus' praise;    50
Like zealous Hermes, who (of all) I said
Most Profits up to all the Gods convaide.
Who, likewise, came into th'Arcadian state
(That's rich in Fountaines, and all celebrate
For Nurse of flocks) where he had vowd a Grove    55
(Surnam'd Cyllenius) to his God-head's love.
Yet even himselfe (although a God he were),
Clad in a squallid sheepskinn governd there
A Mortall's sheepe. For soft Love, entring him,
Conformd his state to his conceipted Trimm,    60
And made him long in an extreame degree
T'enjoy the fayre-hayrd Virgine Dryope.
Which, ere he could, she made him consummate

The florishing Rites of Hymen's honord State,
And brought him such a peece of Progenie                65
As showd (at first sight) monstrous to the eye,
Gote-footed, Two-horn'd, full of noise even then,
And (opposite quite to other children)
Told (in sweete laughter) he ought death no Teare.
Yet strait his Mother start, and fled in feare         70
The sight of so unsatisfying a Thing,
In whose face put forth such a bristled spring.
Yet the most usefull Mercurie embrac't,
And tooke into his armes, his homely-fac't,
Beyond all measure joyfull with his sight;             75
And up to heaven with him made instant flight,
Wrapt in the warme skinne of a Mountaine Hare,
Set him by Jove, and made most merrie fare
To all the Deities else with his Sonne's sight,
Which most of all fill'd Bacchus with delight;         80
And Pan they call'd him, since he brought to All
Of Mirth so rare and full a Festivall.
    And thus, all honor to the shepherds' King!
    For Sacrifice to Thee my Muse shall sing!

## TO VULCAN

    Praise Vulcane, now, Muse; whom Fame gives the Prise
For Depth and Facture of al Fordge devise;
Who, with the skie-eyd Pallas, first did give
Men rules of buildings, that before did live
In Caves and Denns and Hills like savage Beasts;       5
But now, by Art-fam'd Vulcan's Interests
In all their civill Industries, waies cleare

Through th'All-things-bringing-to-their-Ends, the yeare,
They worke out to their Ages' ends, at ease
Lodg'd in safe Roofes from Winter's utmost prease.        10
    But, Vulcan, stand propitious to Me,
    Virtue safe granting, and Felicitie!

### TO PHŒBUS

    O Phœbus! Even the Swann from forth her wings
(Jumping her proyning-banck) thee sweetly sings,
By bright Peneus' whirle-pit-making streames.
Thee that thy Lute mak'st sound so to thy Beames,
Thee, first and last, the sweete-voic't singer still        5
Sings, for thy song's all-songs-transcending Skill.
    Thy Pleasure then shall my song still supply,
    And so salutes thee, King of Poësie.

### TO NEPTUNE

    Neptune, the mighty Marine God, I sing,
Earth's mover, and the fruitles Ocean's king,
That Helicon and th'Ægean Deepes dost hold.
O thou Earth-shaker! Thy Command two-fold
The Gods have sorted, making thee of Horses        5
The awfull Tamer, and of Navall Forces
The sure Preserver. Haile, O Saturns Birth!
Whose gracefull greene hayre circkles all the Earth.
Beare a benigne minde, and thy helpfull hand
Lend All submitted to thy drad Command.        10

## TO JOVE

Jove now I sing, the greatest and the best
Of al these Powrs that are with Deitie blest,
That farr-off doth his dreadfull Voice diffuse,
And (being King of All) doth all conduce
To all their Ends, Who (shut from all Gods else          5
With Themis, that the lawes of all things tells)
Their fit Composures to their Times doth call,
Wedds them together, and preserves This All.
    Grace then, O Farr-heard Jove, the grace t'hast geven,
    Most glorious, and most great of Earth and Heaven.          10

## TO VESTA

Vesta, that (as a servant) Oversees
King Phœbus' hallowd house, in all degrees
Of Guide about it, on the sacred Shore
Of heavenly Pythos, and hast evermore
Rich balms distilling from thy Odorous hayre,          5
Grace this House with thy huswifely repaire!
Enter, and bring a Minde that most may move, ⎤
Conferring even the great in counsailes, Jove; ⎬
And let my verse taste of your either's love. ⎦

## TO THE MUSES AND APOLLO

The Muses, Jove and Phœbus, now I sing;
For from the farr-off-shooting Phœbus spring

All Poets and Musitions, and from Jove
Th'Ascents of Kings. The Man the Muses love,
Felicitie blesses, Elocution's choice                    5
In Syrrup lay'ng, of sweetest breath, his voice.
   Haile, Seede of Jove, my song your honors give,
   And so in Mine shall yours and others' live.


## TO BACCHUS

   Ivie-Crown'd Bacchus Iterate in thy Praises,
O Muse, whose Voice all loftiest Echoes raises;
And He with all th'illustrous seede of Jove
Is joinde in honor, being the fruite of Love
To him and Semele the-great-in-graces;                   5
And from the King his Father's kinde embraces
By faire-hayrde Nymphs was taken to the Dales
Of Nyssa, and with curious Festivals
Given his faire Grought, far from his Father's view,
In Caves from whence eternall Odors flew,               10
And in high number of the Deities plac't.
Yet when the many-Hymne-given God had past
His Nurses' Cares, in Ivies and in Baies
All over Thicketed, his varied waies
To sylvan Coverts evermore he tooke                     15
With all his Nurses, whose shrill voices shooke
Thickets in which could no foote's Entrie fall,
And he himself made Captaine of them All.
   And so, O Grape-abounding Bacchus, be
   Ever saluted by my Muse and Me!                   20
   Give us to spend with spirit our Howres out here,
   And every Howre extend to many a Yeare.

## *TO DIANA*

Diana (that the Golden Spyndle moves,
And loftie soundes as Wel as Bacchus loves,
A bashfull Virgine, and of fearefull hearts
The Death-affecter with delighted Darts,
By Sire and Mother Phœbus' Sister borne,                    5
Whose Thigh the Golden Falchion doth adorne)
I sing; who, likewise over Hills of shade
And Promontories that vast windes invade,
(Amorous of Hunting) bends her all-gold Bowe,
And sigh-begetting Arrows doth bestowe                      10
In fates so dreadfull that the Hill-Tops quake,
And Bristlde woods their leavie foreheads shake,
Horrors invade Earth, and the fishie Seas
Impassiond furies; nothing can appease
The dying Braies of Beasts, and her Delight                 15
In so much Death affects so with affright
Even all inanimate natures. For while shee
Her sports applies, their generall Progenie
Shee all waies turnes upon, to All their Banes.
Yet when her fierie Pleasures finde their wanes,            20
(Her yeelding Bowe unbent) to th'ample House
(Seated in Delphos, rich and Populous)
Of her deare Brother her Retreats advance—
Where th' Instauration of delightsome Dance
Amongst the Muses and the Graces shee                       25
Gives forme; in which her selfe the Regencie
(Her unbent Bowe hung up, and casting on
A gracious Robe) assumes, and first sets gone
The Dance's Entrie; to which all send forth
Their heavenly voices, and advance the worth                30
Of her faire-anckl'd Mother, since to light

Shee Children brought the farr most exquisite
In Counsailes and Performances of all
The Goddesses that grace the heavenly Hall.
    Haile then, Latona's faire-hayrd seede, and Jove's!      35
    My song shall ever call to Minde your Loves.


## TO PALLAS

    Pallas-Minerva's Deitie, the renown'd,
My Muse in her variety must resound;
Mightie in counsailes; whose Illustrous Eyes
In all resemblance represent the skies.
A reverend Maid of an inflexible Minde;      5
In Spirit and Person strong; of Triple kinde;
Fautresse of Cities that just Lawes maintaine;
Of Jove-the-great-in-counsaile's very Braine
Tooke Prime existence; his unbounded Brows
Could not containe her, such impetuous Throws      10
Her Birth gave way to that abrode she flew,
And stood in Gold arm'd in her Father's view,
Shaking her sharpe Lance. All Olympus shooke
So terriblie beneath her that it tooke
Up in amazes all the Deities there;      15
All Earth resounded with vociferous Feare;
The Sea was put up all in purple Waves,
And settld sodainly her rudest Raves;
Hyperion's radiant Sonne his swift-hov'd Steedes
A mighty Tyme staid, till her arming weedes,      20
As glorious as the Gods', the blew-eyd Maid
Tooke from her Deathlesse shoulders. But then staid
All these distempers, and heaven's counsailor, Jove,

Rejoic't that all things else his stay could move.
So I salute thee still; and still in praise                    25
   Thy Fame, and others', shall my Memorie raise.


## TO VESTA AND MERCURIE

   Vesta I sing, who, in Bequest of Fate,
Art sorted out an everlasting State
In all th'Immortals' high-built roofes, and all
Those of Earth-dwelling Men, as generall
And ancient honors given thee for thy gift        5
Of free-liv'd Chastitie and precious Thrift.
Nor can there amongst Mortalls Banquets be
In which, both first and last, they give not Thee
Their endlesse Gratitudes in pourd-out wine,
As gracious sacrifice to thy divine               10
And usefull virtues; being invok't by All,
Before the least Taste of their Festivall
In wine or foode affect their appetites.
And thou that of th'adorn'd with all Delights
Art the most usefull Angell, borne a God          15
Of Jove and Maia, of Heaven's golden Rodd
The sole Sustainer, and hast powre to blesse
With All good All Men, great Argicides,
Inhabit all Good houses, see'ng no wants
Of mutuall mindes' love in th'inhabitants,        20
Joine in kinde blessing with the bashfull Maid
And all-lov'd Virgin, Vesta—either's aid
Combin'd in every Hospitable House,
Both being best seene in all the gracious
House-works of Mortalls. Jointly follow then,     25

Even from their youths, the mindes of dames and men.
   Haile then, ould Daughter of the ouldest God,
   And thou great bearer of Heaven's golden Rodd!
   Yet not to you alone my vowes belong;
   Others as well claime t'Homage of my song.       30


## TO EARTH THE MOTHER OF ALL


   Mother of all things, the well-founded Earth,
My Muse shall memorise; who al the birth
Gives foode that al her upper regions breede,
All that in her divine diffusions feede
In under Continents, all those that live       5
In all the Seas, and All the ayre doth give
Wing'd expeditions, of thy bounties eate;
Faire Children, and faire fruites, thy labor's sweate,
O great in reverence, and referd to thee ⎫
For life and death is all the Pedigree    ⎬   10
Of Mortall humanes. Happie then is He ⎭
Whom the innate Propensions of thy Minde
Stand bent to honor. He shall all things finde
In all abundance; all his Pastures yield
Herds in all plenties; all his roofes are fill'd    15
With rich possessions; He, in all the swaie
Of Lawes best orderd, cuts out his owne way
In Citties shining with delicious Dames,
And takes his choice of all those striving Flames.
High happinesse and riches (like his, Traine)    20
Follow his Fortunes, with delights that raigne
In all their Princes. Glorie invests his Sonnes;
His Daughters, with their croun'd selections

Of all the Cittie, frolick through the Meades,
And every one her calld-for Dances treads          25
Along the soft-flowre of the claver Grasse.
All this, with all those, ever comes to passe
That thy love blesses, Goddesse full of grace,
And treasurous Angell t'all the humane Race.
    Haile then, Great Mother of the Deified kinde,          30
    Wife to the Cope of Starrs! Sustaine a Minde
    Propitious to me for my Praise, and give
    (Answering my minde) my vows fit Meanes to live.


## TO THE SUN

    The radiant Sun's divine renowne diffuse,
Jove's Daughter, great Calliope, my Muse—
Whom Ox-ey'd Euryphaessa gave Birth
To the bright seede of starrie Heaven and Earth.
For the farr-fam'd Hyperion tooke to Wife          5
His Sister Euryphaessa, that life
Of his high Race gave to these lovely Three:
Aurora with the Rosie-wrists, and shee
That ownes th'enamouring tresses, the bright Moone,
Together with the never-wearied Sunne,          10
Who (his Horse mounting) gives both Mortalls light
And all th'immortalls. Even to horror, bright
A blaze burns from his Golden Burgonet,
Which to behold exceeds the sharpest set
Of any eye's intention, beames so cleare          15
It all waies powres abroad The glorious cheare
Of his farr-shining Face up to his Crowne
Casts circular Radiance, that comes streaming downe

About his Temples, his bright Cheeks, and all,
Retayning the refulgence of their Fall.                    20
About his bosome flowes so fine a Weede
As doth the thynnesse of the winde exceede
In rich context; beneath whose deepe folds flie
His Masculine Horses round about the skie,
Till in this Hemisphere he renders staie               25
T'his gold-yo'kt Coch and Coursers; and his way
(Let downe by Heaven) the heavenly Cocheman makes
Downe to the Ocean, where his rest he takes.
  My Salutations then, faire King, receive,
    And in propitious returnes Relieve               30
    My life with Minde-fit means and then from Thee
    And all the race of compleate Deitie
    My song shall celebrate those halfe-God states
    That yet sad death's condicion circulates,
    And whose brave Acts the Gods shew men, that they   35
    As brave may ayme at, since they can but die.


## TO THE MOONE

  The Moone, now, Muses, teach me to resound,
Whose wide wings measure such a world of ground—
Jove's Daughter, deckt with the mellifluous Tongue,
And scene in All the sacred Art of Song;
Whose deathles Brows, when shee from Heaven displaies,   5
All Earth she wraps up in her Orient Raies.
A Heaven of Ornament in Earth is rais'd
When her Beames rise. The subtle Ayre is sais'd
Of delicate splendor from her Crowne of Gold
And, when her silver Bosome is extoll'd,                10

[153]

Washt in the Ocean. In Daies equall'd Noone
Is Mid-night seated; but when shee puts on
Her farr-off-sprinckling-Luster Evening weedes,
(The Moneth in two cut, her high-brested Steedes
Man'de All with curl'd flames, put in Coch and All        15
Her huge Orb fill'd) her whole Trimms then exhall
Unspeakable splendors from the glorious skie.
And out of that State Mortall Men implie
Many Prædictions. And with Heir then
(In Love mixt) lay the King of Gods and Men,               20
By whom (made fruitfull) she Pandea bore
And added, her State to th'immortall Store.
Haile, queene and Goddesse, th'ivorie-wristed Moone
Divine, Prompt, faire-hayr'd. With thy grace begun,
My Muse shall forth and celebrate the praise              25
Of Men whose states the Deities did raise
To Semideities; whose deedes t'endlesse Date
Muse-lov'd and sweete-sung Poets celebrate.


## TO CASTOR AND POLLUX

Jove's faire Sonnes, Father'd by th'Oebalian King,
Muses well-worth-All-Men's-beholdings, sing—
The Deare Birth that Bright-Anckl'd Leda bore,
Horse-taming Castor, and the Conqueror
Of Tooth-tongu'd Momus, Pollux: whom beneath             5
Steepe-Browd Taygetus she gave half-God breath,
In Love mixt with the black-cloudes King of heaven;
Who both of Men and ships (being Tempest driven,
When Winter's wrathfull Empire is in force
Upon th'Implacable Seas) preserve the course.            10

For when the Gusts beginn, (if nere the shore)
The Sea-Men leave their ship, and (evermore
Bearing two milke-white Lambs aboard) they now
Kill them ashore, and to Jove's Issue vow,
When though their ship (in height of all the rore          15
The windes and waves confound) can live no more
In all their hopes; then sodainely appeare
Jove's saving Sonnes, who both their Bodies beare
Twixt yellowe wings, downe from the sparkling Pole,
Who strait the rage of those rude Winds controle,          20
And all the high-waves couch into the Brest
Of t'hoarie Seas. All which sweete signes of rest
To Sea-Men's labors their glad soules conceive,
And End to all their yrckesome grievance give.
   So (once more) to the swift-horse-riding Race          25
   Of Royall Tyndarus, eternall Grace!


## TO MEN OF HOSPITALITIE

   Reverence a Man with use Propitious
That Hospitable rights wants; and a house
(You of this Cittie with the seate of State
To Ox-eyd Juno vowd) yet situate
Nere Pluto's Region—at the extreame Base          5
Of whose so high-hayrd Cittie, from the Race
Of blew-wav'd Hebrus' lovely Fluent, (grac't
With Jove's begetting) you divine Cups Tast.

# BATRACHOMYOMACHIA

# BATRACHOMYOMACHIA

Entring the fields, first let my Vowes call on
The Muses' whole Quire out of Helicon
Into my Heart, for such a Poem's sake
As lately I did in my Tables take,
And put into report upon my knees—                          5
A fight so fierce as might in all degrees
Fit Mars himselfe and his tumultuous hand,
Glorying to dart to th'eares of every land
Of all the voice-devided, and to show
How bravely did both Froggs and Mise bestow             10
In glorious fight their forces, even the deedes
Daring to imitate of earth's Giant seedes.
Thus, then, men talkt; this seede the strife begat:
The Mouse, once drie, and scap't the dangerous Cat,
Drench't in the neighbour lake her tender berde,        15
To taste the sweetnesse of the wave it rer'de.
The farre-fam'de Fen-affecter (seeing him) said:
"Ho! Stranger! what are you? And whence, that tred
This shore of ours? Who brought you forth? Replie
What truth may witnesse, lest I finde you lie.          20
If worth fruition of my love and me,
I'le have thee home, and Hospitalitie
Of feast and gift, good and magnificent,
Bestow on thee. For all this Confluent
Resounds my Royaltie; my Name, the great               25
In blowne-up count'nances and lookes of threat,
Physignathus, ador'd of all Frogs here

---

[9] *Intending Men, being divided from all other creatures by the voice,* μέροψ
*being a periphrasis signifying* voce divisus, *of* μείρω, divido, *and* ὄψ, ὀπός, vox.
　　[27] φυσίγναυος, Genas et buccas inflans.

All their daies' durance, and the Empire beare
Of all their Beings—mine owne Beeing begot
By royall Peleus, mixt in nuptiall knot                    30
With faire Hydromedusa, on the Bounds
Nere which Eridanus his Race resounds.
And Thee mine Eie makes my Conceipt enclinde
To reckon powerfull, both in forme and Minde,
A Scepter-bearer, and past others farre                    35
Advanc't in all the fiery Fights of warre.
Come then, Thy race to my renowne commend."
The Mouse made answer: "Why enquires my friend
For what so well know men and Deities,
And all the wing'd affecters of the skies?                 40
Psicharpax, I am calld, Troxartes' seede,
Surnam'de the Mighty-Minded. She that free'd
Mine eyes from darknesse was Lichomyle,
King Pternotroctes' Daughter, shewing me
Within an aged hovell the young light—                     45
Fed me with figges and nuts, and all the height
Of varied viands, But unfolde the cause,
Why, 'gainst similitude's most equall lawes
(Observ'd in friendship) thou makst me thy friend?
Thy life, the waters only helpe t'extend.                  50
Mine, whatsoever men are us'd to eat
Takes part with them at shore: their purest cheat,
Thrice boulted, kneaded, and subdu'd in past,

[30] Πηλεύς, qui ex luto nascitur.
[31] Ὑδρομέδουσα, Aquarum Regina.
[32] *The river Po, in Italie.*
[41] Ψιχάρπαξ, *Gather-crum, or ravish-crum.*
[41] *Sheare-crust.*
[43] *Lick-mill.*
[44] *Bacon-flitch-devourer, or gnawer.*

In cleane round kymnels, cannot be so fast
From my approches kept, but in I eat;             _  *55*
Nor Cheesecakes full of finest Indian wheat,
That Crustie-weedes weare, large as Ladies' traines;
Lyvrings (white-skind as Ladies); nor the straines
Of prest milke, renneted; nor collups cut
Fresh from the flitch; nor junkets such as put       *60*
Palats divine in Appetite; nor any
Of all men's delicates, though ne're so many
Their Cookes devise them, who each dish see deckt
With all the dainties all strange soiles affect.
Yet am I not so sensuall to flie                  *65*
Of fields embattaild the most fiery crie,
But rush out strait, and with the first in fight
Mixe in adventure. No man with affright
Can daunt my forces, though his bodie bee
Of never so immense a quantitie,              *70*
But making up, even to his bed, accesse,
His fingers' ends dare with my teeth compresse,
His feet taint likewise, and so soft sease both
They shall not tast th'Impression of a tooth.
Sweet sleepe shall hold his owne in every eie     *75*
Where my tooth takes his tartest libertie.
But two there are that alwaies, far and neare,
Extremely still controule my force with feare,
The Cat and Night-Hawke, who much skathe confer
On all the Outraies where for food I erre—       *80*

[57] Τανύπεπλος, Extenso et promisso Peplo amictus. *A metaphor taken from ladies' veiles, or traines, and therefore their names are here added.*

[58] Ἥπατα λευκοχίτωνα, *Livering puddings white skind.*

[64] Παντοδαποῖσιν,—*Whose common exposition is onely* Varijs *when it properly signifies,* Ex omni solo.

Together with the streights-still-keeping Trap,
Where lurkes deceiptfull and set-spleend Mishap.
But most of all the Cat constraines my feare,
Being ever apt t'assault me everywhere;
For by that hole that hope saies I shall scape,                    85
At that hole ever she commits my Rape.
The best is yet, I eat no pot-herb grasse,
Nor Raddishes, nor Coloquintidas,
Nor Still-greene Beeres, nor Parsley—which you make
Your dainties still, that live upon the lake."                     90
The Frog replide: "Stranger, your boasts creepe all
Upon their bellies, though to our lives fall
Much more miraculous meates, by lake and land,
Jove tendring our lives with a twofold hand,
Enabling us to leape ashore for food,                              95
And hide us strait in our retreatfull flood—
Which, if your will serve, you may prove with ease.
I'le take you on my shoulders—which fast sease,
If safe arrivall at my house y'intend."

   He stoopt, and th'other spritelie did ascend,                   100
Clasping his golden necke, that easie seat
Gave to his sallie; who was jocund yet,
Seeing the safe harbors of the King so nere,
And he a swimmer so exempt from Pere.
But when he sunke into the purple wave,                            105
He mournd extremely, and did much deprave
Unprofitable penitence; his haire
Tore by the roots up, labord for the aire,
With his feet fetcht up to his belly close:
His heart within him panted out repose                            110
For th'insolent plight in which his state did stand,

[81] Στονόεσσαν, *of* στενός, *Angustus.*

Sigh'd bitterly, and long'd to greete the land,
Forc't by the dire Neede of his freezing feare.
First, on the waters he his taile did stere
Like to a Sterne, then drew it like an ore,　　　　115
Still praying the Gods to set him safe ashore;
Yet sunke he midst the red waves more and more,
And laid a throat out to his utmost height.
Yet in forc'd speech he made his perill sleight,
And thus his glorie with his grievance strove:　　　120
　　"Not in such choice state was the charge of love
Borne by the Bull, when to the Cretane shore
He swumme Europa through the wavie rore,
As this Frog ferries me, his pallid brest
Bravely advancing, and his verdant crest　　　　125
(Submitted to my seat) made my support,
Through his white waters, to his royall Court."
But on the sudden did apparance make
An horrid spectacle—a water-snake
Thrusting his freckeld necke above the lake.　　　130
Which seene to both, away Physignathus
Div'd to his deepes, as no way conscious
Of whom he left to perish in his lake,
But shunn'd blacke fate himselfe, and let him take
The blackest of it—who amids the Fenn　　　　135
Swumme with his brest up, hands held up in vaine,
Cried "Peepe," and perisht; sunke the waters oft,
And often with his sprawlings calme aloft;
Yet no way kept downe death's relentlesse force,
But (full of water) made an heavie Corse.　　　　140
Before he perisht yet, he threatned thus:
"Thou lurk'st not yet from heaven, Physignathus,
Though yet thou hid'st here, that hast cast from thee
(As from a Rocke) the shipwrackt life of mee.

Though thou thy selfe no better was than I                145
(O worst of things) at any facultie,
Wrastling or race: but for thy perfidie
In this my wracke Jove beares a wreakefull eie,
And to the Hoast of Mise thou paines shalt pay
Past all evasion.' This his life let say,                 150
And left him to the waters. Him beheld,
Lichopinax, plac't in the pleasing fielde,
Who shrick't extremely, ranne and told the Mise;
Who having heard his watry destinies,
Pernicious anger pierst the hearts of all,                155
And then their Heralds forth they sent to call
A councell early, at Troxartes' house,
Sad father of this fatall shipwrack't Mouse,
Whose dead Corpse upwards swum along the lake,
Nor yet (poore wretch) could be enforc'd to make         160
The shore his harbour, but the mid-Maine swum.
When now (all haste made) with first morne did come
All to set councell; in which first rais'd head
Troxartes, angrie for his sonne, and said:
    "O Friends, though I alone may seeme to beare         165
All the infortune, yet may all mette here
Account it their case. But tis true, I am
In chiefe unhappy, that a triple flame
Of life feele put forth in three famous sonnes:
The first, the chiefe in our confusions,                 170
The Cat, made rape of, caught without his hole;
The second, Man, made with a cruell soule,
Brought to his ruine with a new-found sleight,
And a most woodden engine of deceipt,
They terme a Trap, mere Murthresse of our Mise;          175

[152] *Lick-dish.*

The last, that in my love held speciall prise
And his rare mother's, this Physignathus
(With false pretext of wafting to his house)
Strangl'd in chiefe deepes of his bloudy streame.
Come then, haste all, and issue out on them,                    180
Our bodies deckt in our Dædalean armes."
    This said, his words thrust all up in alarmes;
And Mars himselfe, that serves the cure of war,
Made all in their Appropriats circular.
First on each leg the greene shales of a Beane                  185
They clos'd for Bootes, that sat exceeding cleane:
The shales they broke ope, Bootehaling by night,
And eat the beanes. Their Jacks Art exquisite
Had showne in them, being Cats-skins, every where
Quilted with quills. Their fencefull bucklers were              190
The middle rounds of Can'sticks; but their speare
A huge long Needle was, that could not beare
The braine of any but be Mars his owne
Mortall invention. Their heads' arming Crowne
Was vessel to the kirnell of a nut.                            195
And thus the Mise their powers in armour put.
    This the frogs hearing, from the water all
Issue to one place, and a councell call
Of wicked war, consulting what should be
Cause to this murmure and strange mutinie.                     200
While this was question'd, neere them made his stand
An Herald with a Sœpter in his hand
(Embasichytrus calld) that fetcht his kinde
From Tyroglyphus with the mightie minde.
Denouncing ill-nam'd war in these high termes:                201
    "O Frogs! the Mise sends threats to you of armes

[175] Ὀλέτειρα, Interfectrix, Perditrix.
[186] Εὖ τ'ἀσκήσαντες, ab ἀσκέω, Elaboratè concinno.

[165]

And bid me bid ye Battell and fixt fight;
Their eies all wounded with Psicharpax' sight
Floting your waters, whom your king hath kild.
And therefore all prepare for force of field,                    210
You that are best borne whosoever held."
This said, he sever'd; his speech firing th'eares
Of all the Mise, but frees'd the Frogs with feares,
Themselves conceiting guiltie; whom the King
Thus answer'd (rising): "Friends! I did not bring      215
Psieharpax to his end. He, wantoning
Upon our waters, practising to swimme,
Ap'te us, and drown'd without my sight of him.
And yet these worst of Vermine accuse me,
Though no way guiltie. Come, consider we                   220
How we may ruine these deceiptfull Mise.
For my part, I give voice to this advise,
As seeming fittest to direct our deeds:
Our bodies decking with our arming weeds,
Let all our Pow'rs stand rais'd in steep'st repose        225
Of all our shore; that, when they charge us close,
We may the helms snatch off from all so deckt,
Daring our onset, and them all deject
Downe to our waters—who, not knowing the sleight
To dive our soft deeps, may be strangl'd streight,      230
And we triumphing may a Trophey rere
Of all the Mise that we have slaughter'd here."
    These words put all in armes; and mallow leaves
They drew upon their leggs for arming Greaves.
Their Curets, broad greene Beetes; their bucklers were      235

203. *Enter-pot, or Serch-pot.*
204. *Cheese-miner.* Qui caseum rodendo cavat.
218. Μιμούμενος, *Aping or imitating us.*
234. *Boots of warre.*

Good thick-leav'd Cabbadge, proofe gainst any spe're;
Their speares, sharpe Bullrushes, of which were all
Fitted with long ones. Their parts Capitall
They hid in subtle Cockleshels from blowes.
And thus all arm'd, the steepest shores they chose          240
T'encamp themselves, where lance with lance they lin'd,
And brandisht bravelie, each Frogg full of Minde.
   Then Jove calld all Gods in his flaming Throne,
And shewd all all this preparation
For resolute warre—these able soldiers,          245
Many and great, all shaking Iengthfull spe'res,
In shew like Centaures, or the Gyants' Host.
When (sweetlie smiling) he enquir'd who, most
Of all th'Immortalls, pleas'd to adde their aide
To Froggs or Mise; and thus to Pallas said:          250
   "O daughter! Must not you needs aid these Mise,
That, with the Odors and meate sacrifice
Us'd in your Temple, endlesse triumphs make,
And serve you for your sacred victles' sake?"
   Pallas repli'd: "O Father, never I          255
Will aid the Mise in anie miserie.
So many mischiefes by them I have found,
Eating the Cotten that my distaffs crown'd,
My lamps still hanting to devoure the oyle.
But that which most my minde eates is their spoile          260
Made of a veile, that me in much did stand;
On which bestowing an elaborate hand,
A fine woofe working of as pure a thredd,
Such holes therein their Petulancies fed
That, putting it to darning, when t'was done,          265

---

[258] Στέμματα, Lanas, eo quod colus cingant seu coronent. *Which our
learned sect translate eating the crownes that Pallas wore.*

The darner a most deare paie stood upon
For his so deare paines, laid downe instantlie,
Or (to forbeare) exacted usurie.
So, borrowing from my Phane the weed I wove,
I can by no meanes th'usurous darner move                    270
To let me have the mantle to restore.
And this is it that rubs the angrie sore
Of my offence tooke at these petulant Mise.
Nor will I yeeld the Froggs' wants my supplies,
For their infirme mindes that no confines keepe;              275
For I from warre retir'd, and wanting sleepe,
All lept ashore in tumult, nor would staie
Till one winck seas'd myne eyes; and so I laie
Sleeplesse, and pain'de with headach, till first light
The Cock had crow'd up. Therefore, to the fight              280
Let no God goe assistent, lest a lance
Wound whosoever offers to advance
Or wishes but their aid, that skorne all foes,
Should any God's accesse their spirits oppose.
Sit we then pleas'd to see from heaven their fight."         285
   She said, and all Gods join'd in her delight.
And now both Hosts to one field drew the Jarre,
Both Heralds bearing the ostents of warre.
And then the wine-Gnats, that shrill Trumpets sound,
Terriblie rung out the encounter round.                      290
Jove thundred; all heaven sad warr's signe resounded.
   And first Hypsiboas Lichenor wounded,
Standing th'impression of the first in fight.

[268] Τόκος, Partus et id quod partu edidit Mater. Metap. hic appellatur
fœnus, quod ex usura ad nos redit.
   [289] Κώνωψ, Culex vinarius.
   [292] *Lowd-mouth.*
   [292] *Kitchen-vessell licker.*

His lance did in his Lyver's midst's alight,
Along his bellie. Downe he fell; his face            295
His fall on that part swaid, and all the grace
Of his soft hayre fil'd with disgracefull dust.
    Then Troglodytes his thick javeline thrust
In Pelion's bosome, bearing him to ground,
Whom sad death seas'd; his soule flew through his
    wound.                                        300
    Seatlæus next Embasichytros slew,
His heart through thrusting. Then Artophagus threw
His lance at Polyphon, and strooke him quite
Through his midd-bellie: downe he fell upright,
And from his fayre limms took his soule her flight.  305
    Limnocharis, beholding Polyphon
Thus done to death, did, with as round a stone
As that the mill turnes, Troglodytes wound
Neare his mid-neck, ere he his onset found—
Whose eyes sad darknes seas'd Lichenor cast          310
A flying dart off, and his ayme so plac't
Upon Limnocharis, that Sure he thought
The wound he wisht him; nor untruely wrought
The dire successe, for through his Lyver flew
The fatall lance; which when Crambophagus knew,      315
Downe the deepe waves neare shore he, diving, fled;
But fled not fate so; the sterne enimie fed

[298] *Hole-dweller.* Qui foramina subit.
[299] *Mud-borne.*
[301] *Beet-devourer.*
[302] *The great bread-eater.*
[303] *The great Noise-maker, shrill or bigg-voic't.*
[306] *The lake-lover.*
[310] Qui lambit culinaria vasa.
[312] Τιπόσκομαι, intentissime dirigo ut certum ictum inferam.
[315] *The cabbage-eater.*

Death with his life in diving: never more ⎫
The ayre he drew in; his Vermilian gore  ⎬
Staind all the waters, and along the shore ⎭       320
He lay extended; his fat entrailes laie
(By his small guts' impulsion) breaking waie
Out at his wound. Limnisius neare the shore
Destroid Tyroglyphus: which frighted sore
The soule of Calaminth, seeing comming on ⎫    325
(For wreake) Pternoglyphus; who got him gon ⎬
With large leapes to the lake, his Target throwne ⎭
Into the waters. Hydrocharis slew
King Pternophagus, at whose throte he threw
A huge stone, strooke it high, and beate his braine      330
Out at his nostrills: earth blusht with the staine
His blood made on her bosom. For next Prise,
Lichopinax to death did sacrifice
Borborocœtes' faultlesse faculties;
His lance enforc't it; darknes clos'd his eyes.       335
On which when Prassophagus cast his looke,
Cnissodioctes by the heeles he tooke,
Dragg'd him to fenn from off his native ground.
Then seas'd his throate, and souc't him till he droun'd.
  But now Psicharpax wreakes his fellows' deaths,      340
And in the bosome of Pelusius sheathes

[323] Paludis incola, *Lake-liver.*
[325] Qui in Calamintha, herba palustri, habitat.
[326] *Bacon-eater.*
[328] Qui Aquis delectatur.
[329] *Collup-devourer.*
[334] *Mudd-sleeper.*
[336] *Leeke or scalion lover.*
[337] *Kitchin-smell hanter, or hunter.*
[341] *Fennstalker.*

(In center of his Lyver) his bright lance.
He fel before the Author of the chance;
His soule to hell fled. Which Pelobates
Taking sad note of, wreakefully did sease                 345
His hand's gripe full of mudd, and all besmear'd
His forhead with it so, that scarce appeard
The light to him. Which certainely incenst
His fierie splene; who with his wreake dispenst
No point of tyme, but rer'd with his strong hand          350
A stone so massie it opprest the land,
And hurld it at him; when below the knee
It strooke his right legge so impetuouslie
It peece-meale brake it; he the dust did sease,
Upwards everted. But Craugasides                          355
Revendg'd his death, and at his enimie
Dischardg'd a dart that did his point implie
In his mid-bellie. All the sharp-pil'de speare
Got after in, and did before it beare
His universall entrailes to the earth,                    360
Soone as his swolne hand gave his javeline birth.
    Sitophagus, beholding the sad sight
Set on the shore, went halting from the fight,
Vext with his wounds extremelie; and to make
Waie from extreme fate, lept into the lake.               365
    Troxartes strooke, in th'instep's upper part,
Physignathus; who (privie to the smart
His wound imparted) with his utmost hast
Lept to the lake, and fled. Troxartes cast
His eye upon the foe that fell before,                    370

[344] Qui per lutum it.
[355] *Vociferator.*
[362] *Eate-corne.*

[171]

And (see'ng him halfe-liv'de) long'd againe to gore
His gutlesse bosome, and (to kill him quite)
Ranne fiercely at him. Which Prassæus' sight
Tooke instant note of, and the first in fight
Thrust desp'rate way through, casting his keene lance 375
Off at Troxartes, whose shield turn'd th'advance
The sharpe head made, and checkt the mortall chance.
   Amongst the Mise fought an Egregiouse
Young springall, and a close-encountring Mouse,
Pure Artepibulus-his deare descent, 380
A Prince that Mars himselfe shewd where he went
(Call'd Meridarpax), of so huge a might,
That onely He still dominer'd in fight
Of all the Mouse-Host. He, advancing close
Up to the Lake, past all the rest arose 385
In glorious object, and made vant that He
Came to depopulate all the progenie
Of Froggs, affected with the lance of warre.
And certainely he had put on as farre
As he advanc't his vant—he was indude 390
With so unmatcht a force and fortitude—
Had not the Father both of Gods and Men
Instantly knowne it, and the Froggs (even then
Given up to ruine) rescude with remorse:
Who (his head moving) thus began discourse: 395
   "No meane amaze affects me, to behold
Prince Meridarpax rage so uncontrold,
In thirst of Frogg-blood, all along the lake.
Come therefore still, and all addression make,
Dispatching Pallas, with tumultuous Mars, 400

373. *Scallian-devourer.*
380. *Bread-betraier.*
382. *Scrap or broken-meat-eater.*

Downe to the field, to make him leave the wars,
How Potently soever he be said
Where he attempts once to uphold his head."
　Mars answered: "O Jove, neither she nor I
(With both our aides) can keepe depopulacie　　　　405
From off the Froggs. And therefore arme we all,
Even thy lance letting brandish to his call
From off the field, that from the field withdrew
The Titanois, the Titanois that slew,
Though most exempt from match of all earth's seedes,　410
So great and so inaccessible deeds
It hath proclaim'd to men; bound hand and foot
The vast Enceladus, and rac't by th'root
The race of upland Gyants." This speech past,
Saturnius a smoking lightening cast　　　　415
Amongst the armies, thundring then so sore
That with a rapting circumflexe he bore
All huge heaven over. But the terrible ire
Of his dart, sent abroad all wrapt in fire
(Which certainely his very finger was),　　　　420
Amazde both Mise and Froggs. Yet soone let passe
Was all this by the Mise, who much the more
Burnd in desire t'exterminate the store
Of all those lance-lov'd souldiers. Which had beene,
If from Olympus Jove's eye had not seene　　　　425
The Froggs with pittie, and with instant speede
Sent them assistents. Who (ere any heede
Was given to their approch) came crawling on
With Anviles on their backs, that (beat upon
Never so much) are never wearied yet;　　　　430
Crook-pawd, and wrested on with foule cloven feet,

402. Κρατερός, Validus seu potens in retinendo.

Tongues in their mouths, brick-backt, all over bone,
Broade-shoulderd, whence a ruddie yellow shone;
Distorted, and small thigh'd; had eyes that saw
Out at their bosomes; twice foure feet did draw                    435
About their bodies; strong neckt, whence did rise ⎫
Two heads; nor could to any hand be Prise;             ⎬
They call them Lobsters, that eat from the Mise    ⎭
Their tailes, their feet, and hands, and wrested all
Their lances from them so that cold Appall                         440
The wretches put in rout, past all returne.
And now the Fount of light forbore to burne
Above the earth, when (which men's lawes commend)
Our Battaile in one daie tooke absolute end.

#### THE END OF HOMER'S BATTAILE OF FROGGES AND MISE

[429] Νωτάκμονες, Incudes ferentes: *Or Anvile-back't.* Άκμων, Incus, dicta pro syncopen quasi nullis ictibus fatigetur.

[432] Ψαλίδοοστμος, Forcipem in ore habens.

CERTAINE EPIGRAMMS

AND OTHER POEMS OF HOMER

## TO CUMA

Lend hospitable Rights and house-respect,
You that the Virgine with the faire eys deckt
Make Favtresse of your stately-seated Towne
At foot of Sardes, with the high-haird Crowne,
Inhabiting rich Cuma: where ye Taste                    5
Of Hermus' heavenly Fluent, all embrac't
By curld-head whyrlpits, and whose waters move
From the divine seede of immortall Jove.


## IN HIS RETURNE
### To Cuma

Swiftlie my feete sustaine me to the Towne
Where Men inhabit whom due Honors Crowne,
Whose Mindes with free-given faculties are mov'd,
And whose grave Counsailes best of Best approv'd.


## UPON THE SEPULCHER OF MIDUS,
### Cut in Brasse in the
### Figure of a Virgine

A Maid of Brasse I am, Infixed here
T'Eternise Honest Midus' Sepulcher,
And while the streame her fluent seede receives,
And steepe trees curle their verdant brows with leaves,
While Phœbus rais'd above the Earth gives sight,     5
And t'humorous Moone takes Luster from his light,
While floods beare waves, and Seas shall wash the shore,
At this his Sepulcher, whom all deplore,

[177]

I'le constantly Abide, all passers by
Informing: *"Here doth Honest Midus Lie."*                    10


## *CUMA*
### *REFUSING HIS OFFER T'ETERNISE THEIR STATE,*
*though brought thither by the Muses*


O to what Fate hath father Jove given O're
My friendles lite, borne ever to be Pore?
While in my Infant state he pleas'd to save Mee,
Milke on my reverend Mother's knees he gave Me
In delicate and curious Nurserie—                            5
Æolian Smyrna, seated neare the Sea,
(Of glorious Empire, and whose bright sides
Sacred Meletus' silver Current glides)
Being native Seate to me. Which (in the force
Of farr-past Time) the Breakers of wilde Horse,            10
Phriconia's Noble Nation, girt with Towres,
Whose Youth in fight put on with fiery Powres.
From hence, (the Muse-maids, Jove's illustrous seede,
Impelling me) I made impetuous speede,
And went with them to Cuma, with Intent ⎫                   15
T'Eternise all the sacred Continent         ⎬
And State of Cuma. They (in proud Ascent ⎭
From off their Bench) refus'd with usage fierce
The sacred voice which I averre is Verse.
Their follies yet, and madnesse borne by Me,              20
Shall by some Powre be thought on futurely,
To wreake of him whoever whose tongue sought
With false empaire my fall. What fate God brought
Upon my Birth I'le beare with any paine.
But undeserv'd Defame, unfelt, sustaine.                    25

[178]

Nor feeles my Person (deare to me, though Pore)
Any great lust to linger any more
In Cuma's holy Highwaies; but my Minde
(No thought empaird for cares of any kinde
Borne in my body) rather vowes to trie          30
The Influence of any other skie,
And spirits of People bredd in any Land,
Of ne're so slender and obscure Command.


## AN ASSAIE OF HIS BEGUNNE ILIADS

Ilion, and all the brave-Horse-breeding Soile,
Dardania, I sing: that many a Toile
Impos'd upon the Mighty Grecian Powrs,
Who were of Mars the manlie Servitours.


## TO THESTOR'S SONNE,
### *Inquisitive of*
### HOMER
### ABOUT THE CAUSES OF THINGS

Thestorides! Of all the skills unknowne
To errant Mortals, there remains not One
Of more inscrutable Affaire to finde
Than is the true State of a humane Minde.

*Homer intimated in this his Answer to Thestorides—A will to have him learne
the knowledge of himselfe, before hee enquir'd so curiously the causes of other things.
And from hence had the great Peripatetique, Themistius, his most grave Epiphoneme,
Anima quæ seipsam ignorat, quid sciret ipsa de alijs?—and therefore (accord-
ing to Aristotle) advises all Philosophicall Students to beginne with that Studie.*

*Certaine Epigramms*

## *TO NEPTUNE*

Heare, Powreful Neptune, that shak'st Earth in Ire,
King of the great Greene where dance All the Quire
Of faire-hayr'd Helicon; give prosperous Gales
And good passe to these Guiders of our sailes,
Their Voyage rendring happily directed,                    5
And their Returne with no ill Fate affected.
Grant, likewise, at rough Mimas' lowest rootes
(Whose strength up to her Tops prærupt rocks shootes),
My Passage safe arrivall; and that I
My bashfull disposition may applie                         10
To Pious Men, and wreake my selfe upon
The Man whose verball circumvention
In Me did wrong t'Hospitious Jove's whole state,
And t'Hospitable Table violate.

## *TO THE CITTIE ERYTHRÆA*

Worshipfull Earth, giver of all things good!
Giver of even Felicitie, whose flood
The Minde all-over steepes in honey Dewe,       ⎫
That to some Men dost infinite kindenesse shew, ⎬
To others that despise thee art a Shrew,        ⎭       5
And giv'st them Gamesters' galls—who, once their Maine
Lost with an ill chance, fare like Abjects slaine.

## *TO MARINERS*

Ye wave-trod Watermen, as ill as shee
That all the Earth in Infelicitie

[180]

Of Rapine plunges; who upon youre Fare
As sterv'd-like-ravenous as Cormorants are;
The lives ye leade (but in the worse Degree)       5
   Not to be envied more than Misery—
Take shame, and feare the Indignation
Of him that Thunders from the highest Throne,
Hospitious Jove, who at the Back prepares   )
Paines of abhord effect of him that dares    }   10
The Pieties breake of his Hospitious squares. )

## THE PINE

   Any Tree else beares better Fruit than Thee
That Ida's Tops sustaine, where every Tree
Beares up in aire such perspirable Heights,
And in which Caves and sinuous Receipts
Creepe in such great abundance. For about     5
Thy rootes (that ever all thy Fruites put out
As nourisht by them equall with thy Fruites)
Poure Mars his Iron-Mines their accurst pursuites.
So that when any Earth-encroching Man
Of all the Martiall Broode Cebrenian       10
Plead neede of Iron, they are certaine still
About thy Rootes to satiate every Will.

## TO GLAUCUS,
## WHO WAS SO MISERABLIE SPARING THAT
## HE FEARED ALL MEN'S ACCESSE TO HIM

   Glaucus! though wise enough, yet one word more  )
Let my advice add to thy wisedome's store,      }
For t'will be better so. Before thy Dore       )

Give Still thy Mastifs Meate, that will be sure
To lie there, therefore, still, and not endure                    5
(With way-laid eares) the softest foot can fall,
But Men and Beasts make fly Thee and thy stall.


## AGAINST THE SAMIAN MINISTRESSE OR NUNNE

Heare Me, O goddesse, that invoke thine eare,
Thou that dost feede and forme the youthfull Yeare,
And grant that this Dame may the loves refuse
And Beds of Young Men, and affect to use
Humanes whose Temples hoary hayres distaine,           5
Whose Powrs are passing coye, whose Wils would faine.


## WRITTEN ON THE COUNSAILE CHAMBER

Of Men, Sonnes are the Crownes of Citties' Towres;
Of Pastures, Horse are the most bewtious Flowres;
Of Seas, ships are the Grace; and Money still
·With Traines and Titles doth the Family fill.
But Royall Gounsailors, in Counsaile set,                    5
Are Ornaments past All, as clearely great
As Houses are that shining fires enfolde,
Superior farr to Houses nak't and colde.


## THE FORNACE, CALL'D IN TO SING
## BY POTTERS

If ye deale freely, O my fierie Friends,
As ye assure, I'le sing, and serve your Ends.

Pallas! Vouchsafe thou here invok't Accesse,
Impose thy hand upon this Fordge, and blesse
All Cups these Artists earne so, that they may 5
Looke black still with their depth, and every way
Give all their Vessels a most sacred Sale.
Make all well burn'd, and Estimation call
Up to their Prices. Let them marcket well,
And in all high-waies in abundance sell, 10
Till Riches to their utmost wish arise—
And as thou mak'st them rich, so make me wise.
　　But if ye now turne all to Impudence,
And think to pay with lies my Pacience,
Then will I summon gainst your Fornace All 15
Hell's harmefull'st spirits; Maragus I'le call,
Sabactes, Asbett, and Omadamus,
Who ylls against your Art Innumerous
Excogitates, supplies, and multiplies.
Come, Pallas, then, and all command to rise, 20
Infesting Fordge and house with fire, till All
Tumble together and to Ashes Fall,
These Potters' selves dissolv'd in Teares as small.
And as a Horse-cheeke chides his foming Bit,
So let this Fordge murmure in fire and flit, 25
And all this stuffe to ashie ruines runne.
And thou, O Circe, Daughter of the Sunne,
Great-many-Poison-Mixer, come, and poure
Thy cruell'st Poisons on this Potters' floore,
Shivering their vessells; and themselves affect 30
With all the Mischiefes possible to direct
Gainst all their Beings, urdg'd by all thy feends.
Let Chiron likewise come, and all those friends,
The Centaures, that Alcides' fingers fled,
And All the rest too that his hand strooke dead 35

(Their Ghosts excited), come and macerate
These Earthen Men; and, yet with further Fate
Affect their Fornace, all their teare-burst Eyes
Seeing and mourning for their Miseries,
While I looke on, and laugh their blasted Art          40
And them to Ruine. Lastly, if, apart
Any lies lurking, and sees yet, his Face
Into a Cole let th'angrie fire embrace,
That all may learne by them, in all their lust,
To dare Deedes Great, to see them great and Just.    45


## EIRESIONE,
### or
### The Olive Branch


   The Turrets of a Man of infinite Might,
Of infinite Action, substance Infinite,
Wee make accesse to; whose whole Being rebounds
From Earth to Heaven, and nought but Blisse resounds.
Give entrie then, ye Dores; more riches yet          5
Shall enter with me, all the Graces met
In joy of their fruition, perfect Peace
Confirming All—All crown'd with such encrease.
That every emptie Vessell in your House
May stand repleate with all thing precious.        10
Elaborate Ceres may your Larders fill
With all deare Delicates, and serve in still.
May for your Sonne a Wife make wisht approach
Into your Towrs, and rapt in in her Coch
With strong-kneed Mules. May yet her state prove staid   15
With honord Huswiferies, her faire hand laid

To artfull Loomeworks, and her nak't feet treade
The Gumme of Amber to a Golden Beade.
    But I'le returne. Returne, and yet not presse
Your bounties now assaid with oft Accesse,         20
Once a yeere onely, as the Swallow prates
Before the welthie Spring's wide open Gates.
    Meane time I stand at yours, nor purpose stay
More time t'entreate. Give, or not give, away
My feet shall beare me, that did never come      25
With any thought to make your House my Home.


## TO CERTAINE FISHER-BOYES PLEASING HIM
## WITH INGENIOUS RIDDLES

    Yet from the bloods even of your-selfe-like sires
Are you descended, that could make ye heires
To no huge hords of Coine, nor leave ye Able
To feede Flocks of innumerable Rabble.

*THE END OF ALL THE ENDLESS WORKS OF HOMER*

The Worke that I was borne to doe is done.
Glory to Him that the Conclusion
Makes the beginning of my life; and Never
Let me be said to live, till I live Ever.
  Where's the outliving of my Fortunes then,     5
Ye errant vapors of Fame's Lernean Fenn,
That (like possest stormes) blast all not in Herde
With your abhorr'd heads; who, because casher'de
By Men for Monsters, thinck Men Monsters All
That are not of your pyed Hood and your Hall—    10
When you are nothing but the scumm of things, ⎫
And must be cast off—Drones, that have no stings, ⎬
Nor any more soule than a stone hath wings. ⎭
  Avant ye Haggs! Your Hates and Scandalls are ⎫
The Crownes and Comforts of a good Man's Care; ⎬   15
By whose impartiall Perpendiculare, ⎭
All is extuberance and tumor All,
That you your Ornaments and glories call.
Your wrie Mouthes censure right! your blister'd Tongues
That licke but itches, and whose ulcerous Lungs    20
Come up at all things permanent and sound!
O you (like flies in Dreggs) in Humors droun'd,
Your loves, like Atoms, lost in gloomie Ayre,
I would not retrive with a wither'd Haire!
Hate, and cast still your stings then, for your kisses   25
Betray but Truth, and your Applauds are Hisses.
  To see our supercilious wizerds frowne,
Their faces falne like Foggs, and, coming downe,
Stincking the Sunn out, make me shine the more,
And like a checkt flood beare above the shore    30
That their prophane Opinions faine would set

To what they see not, know not, nor can let.
Yet then our learn'd Men with their Torrents come
Roring from their forc't Hills, all crown'd with fome,
That one not taught like them should learne to know        35
Their Greeke rootes, and from thence the Groves that
   grow,
Casting such rich shades, from great Homer's wings,
That first and last command the Muses' springs—
Though he's best Scholler that, through paines and vows
Made his owne Master onely, all things knows.        40
Nor pleades my poore skill forme, or learned Place,
But dantlesse labor, constant Prayer, and Grace.
And what's all their skill but vast varied reading?
As if brode-beaten High-waies had the leading
To Truth's abstract, and narrow Path and Pit,        45
Found in no walke of any worldly wit.
And without Truth, all's onely sleight of hand,
Or our Law-learning in a Forraine Land,
Embroderie spent on Cobwebs, Braggart show
Of Men that all things learne and nothing know.        50
For Ostentation humble Truth still flies,
And all confederate fashionists defies.
And as some sharpe-browd Doctor (English borne)
In much learn'd Latine Idioms can adorne
A verse with rare Attractions, yet become        55
His English Muse like an Arachnean Loome
Wrought spight of Pallas, and therein bewraies
More tongue than truth, beggs, and adopts his Bayes:
So Ostentation, bee hee never so
Larded with labour to suborne his showe,        60
Shall soothe within him but a bastard soule,
No more Heaven heyring than Earth's sonne, the Moule.
But as in dead Calmes emptiest smokes arise

Uncheckt and free, up strait into the skies:
So drousie Peace, that in her humor steepes                    65
All she affects, lets such rise while she sleepes.
Many and most Men have of wealth least store,
But None the gracious shame that fits the Pore;
So most learn'd Men enough are Ignorant,        ⎫
But few the grace have to confesse their want,  ⎬         70
Till Lives and Learnings come concomitant.      ⎭
For from Men's knowledges their Lives'-Acts flowe;
Vaineglorious Acts then vaine prove all they know.
As Night the life-enclining starts best showes,
So lives obscure the starriest soules disclose.               75

    For me, let just Men judge by what I show
In Acts expos'd how much I erre or knowe;
And let not Envie make all worse than nought
With her meere headstrong and quite braineles thought,
Others, for doing nothing, giving All,                         80
And bounding all worth in her bursten Gall.

    God and my deare Redeemer, rescue Me
From Men's immane and mad Impietie,
And by my life and soule (sole knowne to them)
Make me of Palme, or Yew, an Anadem.
And so, my sole God, the thrice sacred Trine,
Beare all th' Ascription of all Me and Mine.

*Supplico tibi, Domine, Pater et Dux rationis nostræ, ut*
*Nostræ Nobilitatis recordemur quâ tu nos ornasti; et ut tu*
*nobis prestò sis, ut iis qui per sese moventur; ut et à Corporis*
*contagio, Brutorumque affectuum repurgemur, eosque*
*superemus, atque regamus; et sicut decet, pro instrumentis iis*    5
*utamur. Deinde, ut nobis Adiumento sis, ad accuratam*
*rationis nostræ correctionem, et coniunctionem cum iis qui*
*verè sunt per lucem veritatis. Et tertiùm, Salvatori supplex*
*oro, ut ab oculis animorum nostrorum, caliginem prorsus*
*abstergas, ut norimus bene qui Deus, aut Mortalis, habendus.*    10
*Amen.*

*SINE HONORE VIVAM, NULLOQUE NUMERO ERO*

*Textual Notes*

# TEXTUAL NOTES

## Dedication

### Heading

| | |
|---|---|
| MOST-WORTHIE-TO-BE- MOST-HONOR'D | MOST-WORTHIE-TO-BE-MOST HONOR'D |
| 26 *to Heaven* | [The Harvard copy is corrected: to All Heauen] |
| 66 *Springs* | Spring's |
| 85 *th'House* | T'House |
| 90 *th'Enimies'* | Th' Enimies |
| 91 *and* | & |
| *and* | & |
| 111 *from hence* | frõ hẽce |
| 127 *men, and* | mẽ; & |

## The Occasion

| | |
|---|---|
| 2 and | & |
| 11 drowning | *deuouring* [manuscript correction by Chapman in the Harvard copy] |
| 14 Hymns | *Hymn's* |
| 19 Hymns | *Hym'ns* |
| 26 our ever-the-Same | *our-euer-the Same* |

## An Hymne to Apollo

### Heading

| | |
|---|---|
| Hymne | Hymne |
| 45 lands | *land* |
| 49 or | *Or* |
| 50 or | *Or* |
| 52 or | *Or* |
| 64 that | *That* |
| 70 if | *If* |
| 82 or | *Or* |
| 98 nor | *Nor* |

| | | |
|---|---|---|
| | thee | *theee* |
| 135 | Rhea | Rhæa |
| 137 | every | *Euery* |
| 192 | every | *Euery* |
| 237 | who | *Who* |
| 247 | songs | *song's* |
| 279 | both | *Both* |
| 296 | th' | *Th'* |
| 338 | passing | *Passing* |
| 340 | Perrhæbes | Perrhabes |
| 347 | Euripus | Eurypus |
| 351 | Teumessus | Teucmessus |
| 383 | Cephissus | Cephyssus |
| 385 | Lilæus | Lylæus |
| 398 | even | *Euen* |
| 399 | Peloponnesus | Peloponesus |
| 404 | the | *The* |
| 415 | th' | *Th'* |
| 430 | Parnassus | Paranassus |
| 439 | his | *His* |
| 445 | Cephissus' | Cephyssus |
| 448 | the with-snowe-still-croun'd | *the-with-snowe-still croun'd* |
| 458 | Peloponnesus | Peloponessus |
| 460 | that | *That* |
| 483 | having | *Hauing* |
| 486 | whom | *Whom* |
| 513 | Her | *her* |
| 528 | Titanois | Titanoys |
| 543 | Dædalian | Dedalian |
| 582 | Chimæra | Chymæra |
| 595 | to | *To* |
| 599 | frauds | *fraud's* |
| 601 | it | *It* |
| 618 | Cnossus | Gnossus |
| 628 | Pylian | Pylean |
| 638 | but | *But* |
| 639 | and | *And* |
| 641 | Malean | Mal    e |

| | | |
|---|---|---|
| 644 | a | *A* |
| 647 | on | *On* |
| 654 | or | *Or* |
| 656 | Peloponnesian | Peloponesian |
| 659 | and | *And* |
| 660 | Argyphæa | Aryphæa |
| | and | *And* |
| 666 | and | *And* |
| 667 | all | *All* |
| 673 | Peloponnesus | Peloponesus |
| | and | *And* |
| 675 | Morea | Moræa |
| 694 | in | *In* |
| 698 | like | *lik* |
| | againe | *Againe* |
| 705 | or | *Or* |
| 706 | conferring | *Conferring* |
| 710 | nor | *Nor* |
| 732 | Cnossus | Gnossus |
| 759 | a | *A* |
| 778 | fire | *Fire* |
| 783 | food | *foot* |
| 788 | all | *All* |
| 799 | that all | *that All* |
| 815 | your | *yonr* |
| 824 | all | *All* |
| 827 | If | [new paragraph] |
| 831 | Besides | [new paragraph] |
| 833 | all | *All* |

## A Hymne to Hermes

| | | |
|---|---|---|
| 2 | and | *&* |
| 5 | the | *The* |
| 16 | and | *And* |
| 28 | he | *He* |
| 38 | since | *Since* |
| | he | *He* |

| | | |
|---|---|---|
| 54 | borne | *Borne* |
| 58 | from | *From* |
| 76 | or | *Or* |
| 97 | And | *and* |
| 124 | all | *All* |
| 153 | the | *The* |
| 156 | past | *Past* |
| 174 | that | *That* |
| 179 | but | *But* |
| 202 | which | *Which* |
| 222 | he | *He* |
| 250 | and | *And* |
| 260 | all | *All* |
| 268 | whirle-pit-eating flood | *whirle-pit-eating-flood* |
| 270 | The that-morne-borne Cyllenius | *The-that-morne-borne-Cyllenius* |
| 274 | His borne-to-barke mouth | *His-borne-to-barke-mouth* |
| 283 | in | *In* |
| 316 | now | *Now* |
| 346 | Ocean great-in-ebbs-and-flows | *Ocean-great-in-ebbs-and flows* |
| 349 | round-and-long-neckt | *round and long-neckt* |
| 368 | if | *If* |
| 396 | and | *And* |
| 420 | on | *On* |
| 422 | as | *As* |
| 425 | even | *Euen* |
| 432 | and | *And* |
| 435 | his | *His* |
| 436 | as | *As* |
| 439 | and | *And* |
| 441 | weeds | *weed's* |
| 442 | shrouds | *shroud's* |
| 444 | in | *In* |
| 447 | a | *A* |
| 449 | thus | *Thus* |
| 451 | instantly | *Instantly* |
| 453 | or | *Or* |

# Textual Notes

| | | |
|---|---|---|
| 469 | could | *Could* |
| 470 | or | *Or* |
| 472 | that | *That* |
| 491 | that | *That* |
| 493 | nor | *Nor* |
| 495 | What | *what* |
| 496 | Knowes | *knowes* |
| 521 | Up | *up* |
| 541 | my | *My* |
| 560 | or | *Or* |
| 570 | and | *And* |
| 571 | he | *He* |
| 573 | nor | *Nor* |
| 604 | such | *Such* |
| 607 | Oblivion-marckt whole | *Obliuion-marckt-whole* |
| 614 | all | *All* |
| 619 | heaps | *heap's* |
| 622 | that | *That* |
| 662 | using | *Vsing* |
| 693 | in | *In* |
| 746 | and | *&* |
| 752 | in | *In* |
| 792 | And | *and* |
| 802 | here | *Here* |
| 806 | and | *And* |
| 814 | Without | *without* |
| 818 | and | *And* |
| 868 | Let | *let* |
| 873 | However cunning-hearted | *How-euer-cunning hearted* |
| 878 | which | *Which* |
| 891 | which | *Which* |
| 903 | Goods | *Gods* |
| 904 | curving | *cumming* |

## *A Hymne to Venus*

| | | |
|---|---|---|
| 10 | Ægis-bearing Jove | *Ægis-bearing-*Ioue |
| 19 | and | *&* |

[197]

| | | |
|---|---|---|
| 27 | but | *But* |
| 73 | Rhea | *Rhæa* |
| 88 | but | *But* |
| 95 | Ida's top-on-top-to-heav-en's-Pole-heapt | *Idas-top-on-top-to-heauens-Pole heapt* |
| | [note] verticem | *virticem* |
| 110 | All-of-GoId-made laughter-loving | *All-of-Gold-made-laughter-louing* |
| 123 | Denns, obscur'd | *Denns-obscur'd* |
| 126 | in | *In* |
| 137 | high-taken heeds | *high-taken-heed's* |
| 172 | Troyan | Troian |
| 181 | Why | *why* |
| 184 | if | *If* |
| 189 | it | *It* |
| 190 | Troyan | Troian |
| 199 | and | *&* |
| 201 | all | *All* |
| 205 | Golden-Rodd-sustaining Argus' | *Golden-Rodd-sustaining-*Argus |
| 214 | and | *And* |
| 224 | brought | *broisght* |
| 269 | Unbutton'd | *Vnbutto'nd* |
| 296 | if | *If* |
| 324 | Troyans | Troians |
| 362 | sustain'd | *stustain'd* |
| 367 | Tithon | Tython |
| 417 | all | *All* |
| 426 | Nymphs | *Nymps* [the Harvard copy reads, correctly: *Nymphs*] |
| 475 | to | *te* |

## To the Same

| | | |
|---|---|---|
| 3 | where | *Where* |
| 4 | Zephyr | Zephire |
| 10 | Weeds | *Weed's* |
| 13 | of | *Of* |

# *Textual Notes*

## Bacchus

|   |   |   |
|---|---|---|
| 3 | prominent | *prominẽt* |
| 19 | therefore strait | *therefore-strait* |
| 31 | or | *Or* |
| 32 | or | *Or* |
| 47 | his | *His* |
| 71 | obscure-greene Ivie's | *obscure-greene-Iuies* |
| 87 | but | *But* |
| 92 | inspired | *inspir'd* |
|   | in | *In* |

## To Mars

|   |   |   |
|---|---|---|
| 1 | Mars, Most-strong | *MArs-Most-strong* |
| 8 | that | *That* |
| 9 | to | *To* |
| 11 | Pleiads | Pleiad's |

## To Diana

|   |   |   |
|---|---|---|
| 2 | and | *&* |
| 4 | all-of-Gold-made Chariot | *all of Gold-made-Chariot* |
| 9 | where | *Where* |

## To Venus

|   |   |   |
|---|---|---|
| 3 | that | *That* |

## To Pallas

|   |   |   |
|---|---|---|
| 1 | onely | *Onely* |

## To Juno

|   |   |   |
|---|---|---|
| 2 | Rhea | Rhæa |
| 4 | of | *Of* |

## To Ceres

|   |   |   |
|---|---|---|
| 7 | Keepe | *keepe* |

# Textual Notes

## To Lyon-hearted Hercules

| 1 | Alcides | ALlcides |
| 6 | and | *And* |
| 15 | Vouchsafe | *vouchsafe* |

## To Pan

| 5 | that | *That* |
| 23 | so | *So* |
| 55 | where | *Where* |
| 67 | then | *Then* |

## To Vulcan

| 2 | and | & |

## To Phœbus

| 3 | whirle-pit-making streames | *whirle-pit-making-streames* |
| 6 | song's all-songs-transcending | *songs-all-songs-transcending* |

## To Neptune

| 2 | and | *&* |
| 3 | Ægean Deepes | Ægan *Depees* |

## To Jove

| 1 | and | *&* |
| 10 | and | *&* |
| | and | *&* |

## To Bacchus

| 5 | Semele the-great-in-graces | Semele-*the-great-in-graces* |

## To Diana

| 13 | the fishie | fishie |
| 18 | their | *Their* |
| 24 | th' | *Th'* |
| 26 | in | *In* |
| 35 | and | *&* |

# *Textual Notes*

## *To Pallas*

| | | |
|---|---|---|
| 10 | Throws | *Throw's* |
| 13 | All | *all* |
| 22 | But | *but* |

## *To Vesta and Mercurie*

| | | |
|---|---|---|
| 3 | and | *&* |
| 4 | as | *As* |
| 20 | th' | *Th'* |
| 30 | t' | *T'* |

## *To Earth*

| | | |
|---|---|---|
| 5 | all | *All* |
| 7 | of | *Of* |
| 14 | all | *All* |
| 15 | all | *All* |
| 31 | Sustaine | *sustaine* |

## *To the Sun*

| | | |
|---|---|---|
| 12 | th' | *Th'* |
| 15 | beames | *Beames* |
| 31 | and | *&* |

## *To the Moone*

| | | |
|---|---|---|
| 13 | farr-off-sprinckling-Luster Evening | *farr-off-sprinckling-Luster-Euening* |
| 16 | then | *Then* |
| 21 | Pandea | Pandæa |
| 23 | and | *&* |

## *To Castor and Pollux*

| | | |
|---|---|---|
| 1 | th' | Th' |
| 2 | a Muses well-worth-All-Men's-beholdings | *Muses-well-worth-All Mens beholdings* |
| 3 | Leda | Læda |
| 22 | t' | *T'* |

# Textual Notes

## To Men of Hospitalitie

5  at                     *At*

## Batrachomyomachia

| | | |
|---|---|---|
| 9 | and | *And* |
| 19 | Who | *who* |
| | Replie | *replie* |
| 22 | I'le | *Ile* |
| 27 | [note] et | *&* |
| 28 | and | *And* |
| 29 | mine | *Mine* |
| 31 | on | *On* |
| 35 | and | *And* |
| 38 | Why | *why* |
| 41 | Psicharpax | Psycharpax |
| 57 | [note] et | *&* |
| 59 | nor | Nor |
| 60 | nor | *Nor* |
| 62 | though | *thought* |
| 64 | [note] *common* | commõ |
| 74 | th' | *Th'* |
| 88 | Coloquintidas | *Coloquintida's* |
| 98 | I'le | *Ile* |
| 100 | th'other | *thither* |
| 107 | his | *His* |
| 124 | his | *His* |
| 167 | tis | *ti's* |
| 181 | Dædalean | Dedalean |
| 197 | from | *From* |
| 208 | Psicharpax' | Psycharpax |
| 216 | Psicharpax | Psycharpax |
| 225 | Pow'rs | *'Powr's* |
| 229 | who | *Who* |
| 234 | [note] *Boots* | Boot's |
| 245 | these | *These* |
| 292 | Lichenor | Lychenor |
| 301 | Seutlæus | Sentlæus |

| | | |
|---|---|---|
| 302 | Then | *then* |
| 306 | Limnocharis | Lymnocharis |
| 310 | Lichenor | Lychenor |
| 312 | Limnocharis | Lymnocharis |
| 315 | Crambophagus | Crambaphagus |
| 323 | Limnisius | Lymnisius |
| 336 | Prassophagus | Brassophagus |
| 336 | [note] Leeke or | Leeke-or |
| 337 | Cnissodioctes | Cnisodioctes |
| 340 | Psicharpax | Psycharpax |
| 364 | and | *And* |
| 377 | and | *&* |
| 382 | of | *Of* |
| 432 | brick-backt | *Brick-backt* |
| | all | *All* |
| 435 | twice | *Twice* |
| 436 | strong | *Strong* |
| 443 | when | *When* |

## *To Cuma*

| | | |
|---|---|---|
| 7 | and | *And* |

## *Upon the Sepulcher of Midus*

| | | |
|---|---|---|
| 6 | t' | *T'* |
| 9 | all | *All* |

## *Cuma refusing his Offer*

| | | |
|---|---|---|
| 1 | to | *To* |
| 24 | I'le | *Iile* |

## *To Thestor's Sonne*

| | | |
|---|---|---|
| 1 | [note] *the* | *The* |
| 4 | [note] *and* | *And* |

## *To Neptune*

| | | |
|---|---|---|
| 14 | t' | *T'* |

# Textual Notes

## To the Cittie Erythræa

| | | |
|---|---|---|
| 7 | chance | *cãhce* |

## To Mariners

| | | |
|---|---|---|
| 1 | as | *As* |
| 3 | who | *Who* |

## The Pine

| | | |
|---|---|---|
| 11 | they | *They* |

## The Fornace

| | | |
|---|---|---|
| 28 | Great-many-Poison-Mixer | *Great-many-Poison Mixer* |
| 38 | all | *All* |
| 40 | on | *On* |

## Eiresione

| | | |
|---|---|---|
| 4 | and | *&* |
| 6 | all | *All* |
| 16 | her | *Her* |

## [Final verses]

| | | |
|---|---|---|
| 2 | Him | *him* |
| 14 | Your | *your* |
| 17 | tumor | *excretion* |
| 26 | Applauds | *Applaud's* |
| 36 | and | *&* |
| 40 | knows | *know's* |

## [Latin prayer]

| | | |
|---|---|---|
| 6 | *Adiumento* | Adiuneto |

*Commentary*

# COMMENTARY

## The Occasion

24–27 notwithstanding
... Impiety

I take this as meaning: "in spite of the fact that all men, servile and hidebound in their opinions, miserably ignored his great and unequalled merit, while at the same time they overflowed in their welcome of imposture and impiety."

## An Hymne to Apollo

113 for penurie of Men
"Because of the lack of men," translating χήτεϊ λαῶν.

117–18 to render ... they fall
"To prophesy coming events" when men demand an oracle.

147 Thaumantia
Iris.

224 Sweet
In all probability this is "suite," so spelt to rime with "feet."

227 Champion fight
Evidently "boxing," translating πυγμαχίη.

289 that sounds ... set gone
"Which sends its harmonies up to heaven."

401 Whom future ... brings
"Who are brought here in search of information concerning the future."

422 in his pleasure's place
"In the place of this pleasure."

473 built for eternall date
"Built to last for ever."

563–64 that invok't ... gave
Apparently this simply means, "which brought death, as he had intended it to."

579–81 Now from thee ... death
This translates οὐδὲ τί τοι θανατόν γε δυσηλεγέ' οὔτε Τυφωεὺς ἀρκέσει οὔτε Χίμαιρα δυσώνυμος, and seems to mean "Neither Typhon nor Chimæra will be of any power to avert death from you."

# Commentary

| | | |
|---|---|---|
| 645 | Heaven's Comforter of sight | The Sun. |
| 655 | it failde t'obay | "The ship failed to answer to the rudder." |
| 714 | that with . . . stand | "Which their health and stomachs need." |
| 732–34 | Yet no more . . . Iov'd Cittie | "Yet you must return no more to your beloved city." |
| 734–35 | severalls . . . and houses | "Your individual wives and houses." |
| 829–30 | Know that . . . sustaine | It is almost impossible to determine what precisely Chapman meant here. The original text says that they will lose their privileges and be subdued. |

## A Hymne to Hermes

| | | |
|---|---|---|
| 14 | when great . . . consummate | "When the purpose of great Jove was fulfilled." |
| 19 | Could turne . . . assaies | "Could turn and twist so as to bring about what he desired." |
| 21–22 | bore a varied finger | Evidently this means "had various devices." |
| 49–51 | Which . . . wit | Apparently meaning, "which your ill form will not prevent me, by my skill, from making use of you." |
| 136 | Thirsting . . . height | "Anxious to attempt some extraordinary thing." |
| 144 | In ayre's . . . Abods | This simply means, "they dwelt in the open air." |
| 167–69 | but as . . . needing it | Here Chapman seemingly got lost in the Greek text, οἷά τ᾽ ἐπειγόμενος δολιχήν ὁδόν, αὐτοτροπήσας—which is confessedly puzzling. Presumably he intended the meaning to be, "but as if he were merely collecting food for his journey, since he had a long way to go and needed to carry provisions with him." |

# Commentary

| | | |
|---|---|---|
| 249–50 | and his owne . . . due | Once again Chapman seems to have been uncertain about what he intended to express. |
| 267 | a novell voice's note | Presumably, "a new device." |
| 326–27 | being . . . Acres | The sense is clear, but the grammar—and the precise usage of "reapes"—is obscure: "having the benefit of the corn cut in a great number of acres." |
| 343 | the Gote-hyde-wearer's Sonne | The son of Zeus. |
| 353–54 | whom Latona's . . . strange | "Whom Apollo did not refrain from saluting." |
| 388 | That strooke but one plaine | It is to be suspected that Chapman could make no clear sense of the Greek, ὃ δὲ θᾶσσον ὁδὸν κίε μῦθον ἀκούσας· οἰωνὸν δ᾿ ἐνόει τανυσίπτερον, αὐτίκα δ᾿ἔγνω φηλητὴν γεγαῶτα Διὸς παῖδα Κρονίωνος. |
| 435 | Chace | Probably, "closely concealing the theft of the oxen." |
| 468 | a false Relation faine | "Present a false report." |
| 603 | After . . . infinite space | "After I had travelled far." |
| 612–13 | being so . . . in doubt | "Being so skilfully designed to deceive." |
| 629 | got his Passe sign'd | "Finished his journey." |
| 658 | Bliss-indu'd | "Gods." |
| 763–64 | as it . . . Birth | "According to their order of age and birth." |
| 826 | And even . . . earne | "And no sooner do you desire it than it is done." |
| 853–54 | even when . . . sing | "Even when he aims at singular virtue in what he plays or sings." |
| 904 | curving | The text reads *"cumming,"* but presumably Chapman wrote *"curving,"* translating καμπύλα τόξα. |
| 905–06 | what . . . witnesse | "Would take the oath the Gods use." |
| 921 | Gifts of Deitie | "Divine gifts." |

# Commentary

## A Hymne to Venus

| | | |
|---|---|---|
| 153–54 | the Deity that Darts affecteth | Artemis. |
| 154–55 | that gave the eye of Heaven his heat | Latona (Leto). |
| 155–56 | that moves The hearts of all | Venus. |
| 157 | the blew-eyd Maid | Athene. |
| 171–72 | give me . . . hearts | "Make the Trojans love me." |
| 197–98 | her . . . shafts | Artemis. |
| 201–02 | all circkl'd . . . Multitude | "Surrounded by a large crowd," translating ἀμφὶ δ᾽ ὅμιλος ἀπείριτος ἐστεφάνωτο. |
| 208 | a labour of Mortalitie | "A work of man," translating πολλὰ δ᾽ ἔπ᾽ ἤγαγεν ἔργα καταθνητῶν ἀνθρώπων. |
| 212 | On her . . . comforted | The earth. |
| 299 | he enjoy'd his eare | "He listened." |

## Bacchus

| | | |
|---|---|---|
| 55 | Since that Prise . . . let fall | Apparently, "since some God certainly put this prize in our way"—ἐπεὶ ἡμῖν ἔμβαλε δαίμων. |

## To Pan

| | | |
|---|---|---|
| 70 | Start | "Started." |

## To Earth

| | | |
|---|---|---|
| 23 | with their croun'd selections | "With the suitors whom they have chosen." |

## To the Moone

| | | |
|---|---|---|
| 2 | Whose wide . . . ground | Translating "long-winged," τανυσίπτερον. |

# Commentary

## Batrachomyomachia

| | | |
|---|---|---|
| 91–92 | your boasts . . . bellies | "Your boasts are all concerned with matters relating to the stomach"— translating λίην αὐχεὶς ἐπὶ γαστέρι. |
| 100 | th'other | The text reads "thither," but the sense needs a definite reference to the mouse. |
| 106–07 | did much . . . penitence | "Did much, unprofitably, blame himself for the penance he was undergoing." etc. |
| 111 | in which his state did stand | "In which he found himself." |
| 119–20 | Yet in forc'd speech . . . strove | "Yet when he did speak, he minimised his sense of danger, since his desire to be esteemed brave strove with his fear." |
| 150 | Past all evasion | "However much you try to evade them." |
| 154 | his watry destinies | "His fatal end in the water." |
| 170 | the chief in our confusions | "Our principal bane." |
| 184 | Made all . . . circular | "Equipped them all completely in appropriate armour." |
| 192–93 | that could not beare the braine of any | "That could not have been invented by any brain." |
| 218 | without my sight of him | "Without my seeing him," translating οὐδὲ κατεῖδον ὀλλύμενον. |
| 261 | that me in much did stand | "That I much valued," or "On which I had devoted much toil." |
| 266–71 | The darner . . . mantle to restore | It is doubtful whether Chapman himself knew precisely what he wanted to express here. The sense of the original is that Pallas had borrowed money in order to make the veil and now cannot repay:— |

$$\delta \; \delta' \dot{\eta} \pi \eta \tau \acute{\eta} \varsigma \; \mu o \iota \; \dot{\epsilon} \pi \acute{\epsilon} \sigma \tau \eta$$
$$\kappa \alpha \grave{\iota} \; \pi \rho \acute{\alpha} \sigma \sigma \epsilon \iota \; \mu \epsilon \; \tau \acute{o} \kappa o \nu \ldots$$
$$\chi \rho \eta \sigma \alpha \mu \acute{\epsilon} \nu \eta \; \gamma \grave{\alpha} \rho \; \ddot{\upsilon} \varphi \alpha \nu \alpha \; \kappa \alpha \grave{\iota} \; o \dot{\upsilon} \kappa \; \ddot{\epsilon} \chi \omega$$
$$\dot{\alpha} \nu \tau \alpha \pi o \delta o \tilde{\upsilon} \nu \alpha \iota.$$

# Commentary

| | | |
|---|---|---|
| 280–84 | Therefore, to the fight . . . oppose | The general sense is: "Let no god assist in the fight, for if he enters the battle or even just tries to aid them, they are so fierce against their enemies that they might dare to attack him." |
| 293 | Standing . . . fight | "Meeting the first shock of the foe." |
| 295–96 | his face . . . swaid | "He fell on his face." |
| 361 | Soone as . . . birth | I have no idea what Chapman intends here. |
| 402–03 | How Potently . . . his head | Another of Chapman's peculiarly involved phrases, meaning—it would seem—simply: "However powerfully he may fight." |
| 408 | That | Refers to *thy lance*: "getting him out of the battle by using the lance that slew the Titans." |

## To Cuma

| | | |
|---|---|---|
| 6–7 | all embrac't . . . whyrlpits | Since Chapman is fond of using the word "whirlpit" in connection with streams, it is interesting to note that the whole phrase here means nothing more than "eddying," διυήεντος. |

## [Final verses]

| | | |
|---|---|---|
| 17 | Tumor | Chapman's own correction of *"excretion"* in the printed text. |

*Glossary*

# GLOSSARY

So STRANGE became Chapman's use of language that there are scores of words and phrases which, in bold terms or more subtly, appear in these translations with significances not commonly assigned to them. The present glossary aims merely at giving aid to the reader of the poems, with an asterisk indicating usages or meanings for which he individually seems to have been responsible. Included also are words spelt, often for rime's sake, in peculiar ways.

| | |
|---|---|
| abject | abject creature |
| abode | [This is frequently used in peculiar phrases, as in "solac't Abods," meaning "dwelt"] |
| absolute | complete, perfect |
| access | entry, movement towards, approach |
| acquite | acquit |
| address | 1) bring forward |
| | 2) skill, effort (as in "thine own address," meaning "your own efforts") |
| addression | direction of one's course |
| admire | wonder at |
| advance | put forward (as in "that they advanc't to her," meaning "which they built for her") |
| adversively | * adversely, in an opposite direction |
| affect | 1) turn towards (as in "whose face affects the west") |
| | 2) possess (as in "whose flood affects so many silver streames") |
| | 3) touch, or infect |
| | 4) effect |
| affected | 1) touched |
| | 2) afflicted (as in "affected with the lance of war") |
| affecter | one who has an affection for, user |
| all-else | * all other |
| ambient | revolving |
| amends | dowry (as in "in my Amends," meaning "as a dowry") |
| amplified | ["Amplified past others" means "outstanding"] |

# Glossary

| | |
|---|---|
| angel | 1) messenger |
| | 2) blesser, protector |
| antipathy | * anything opposite to another |
| appall | fear |
| apparance | appearance |
| appose | place to or on |
| appropriats | * appropriate things |
| approve | declare |
| ap'te | aped |
| arrive | cause to arrive |
| as | [Frequently meaning "as if"] |
| ascend | rise to, attain |
| attoned | reconciled |
| attraction | * ornament |
| autentique | authentic |
| author | 1) originate, be the cause of |
| | 2) one who originates anything |
| ayre | air (often used as "wind") |
| beam | * [Used in various senses, once evidently as "song"] |
| bear . . . a finger | [See Commentary, *A Hymne to Hermes*, ll. 21–22] |
| belluine | * the race of animals |
| bene | been |
| bequest | that which is bestowed ("in Bequest of Fate" means "according to fate's decrees") |
| berde | beard |
| beseeging | besieging (sometimes used almost in the sense of "afflicting") |
| birth | race, animals |
| blame | blaming ("of his blame" means "of what he accuses me") |
| blone | blown |
| blore | gale |
| bolle | bowl |
| boote haling | carrying away of booty, foraging |
| borne | born |
| broch | * broach, branch |
| bryre | briar |
| burgonet | helmet |
| can'stick | candlestick |

[216]

# Glossary

| | |
|---|---|
| carquenet | carcanet, chain of jewels |
| cautelous | wily |
| cheat | bread |
| chrimsine | crimson |
| circular | complete, perfect |
| circularly | completely |
| circulate | encircle, bind |
| circumflex | bending round |
| circumvention | [Used in a peculiar phrase, "verbal circumvention in me," meaning "deceiving me"] |
| claver grass | clover |
| clear | noble |
| close | secret (as in "close Heart") |
| closset | close or secret place, lair |
| clymes | [In *Hermes*, II. 552–53 "the Clymes of rapture," the word may be intended for either "climes" or "climbs"] |
| coch | coach |
| collateral | equal, corresponding |
| coloquintida | bitter apple |
| come up at | attack |
| composure | * fulfillment |
| conceipt | conceit |
| conceit | think, consider |
| conclude | * [In *Hermes*, II. 659–60 "conclude his bare assertion," the word seems to mean "back up, support"] |
| concomitant | concurrent |
| confer | *1) agree or harmonise with (in *Vesta*, I. 8 "conferring . . . Jove" translates ἔν᾽ ἔρχεο θυμὸν ἔχουσα σὺν Διὶ μητιόεντι) *2) bring, impose (as in "conferring wrongs") |
| confluent | * water, pond (without any implication of streams flowing together) |
| contendresse | one who urges her way or hastens towards (as in "for Troy became a swift Contendresse") |
| contention | endeavour (in *Pan*, I. 37 "contention of song" means simply "melody, chant") |
| contumelious | presumptuous, insolent (translating ὑβριστάων) |

# Glossary

| | |
|---|---|
| convert | turn or turn to (as in "convert recourse to") |
| cornel | [In *Hermes*, I. 803 "cornel dart" apparently means "cornelled" or "embattled"] |
| counterprise | * comparison ("bear the Counterprise" means "be compared with") |
| covetous | eager, striving, involving competition (as in "covetous sport of getting glory") |
| crown | 1) end, conclusion |
| | 2) chief effort |
| | 3) ring (of people) |
| crustie-weeds | * [Apparently the frillings on a cake] |
| cure | care (as in "cure of war") |
| Dædalian | ingenious, formed by art ("Dædalian Throne" translates πολυδαίδαλον) |
| date | duration ("long date" means "a long time," "endless date" is "eternity" and "to endless date" is "continually") |
| deceiptfull | deceitful |
| dehort | exhort against |
| deified | divine |
| deject | cast down |
| delighted | affording delight |
| delightsome | delighted |
| den | make a den |
| denounce | announce (as in "denouncing ill-nam'd war") |
| depopulacy | * depopulated condition, depopulation |
| deposition | placing or putting down |
| deprave | vilify, abuse (but it is difficult to give an exact meaning for the word as used in *Batrachomyomachia*, II. 106–7, "did much deprave Unprofitable penitence") |
| desire | satisfaction (as in "to her desire") |
| disgraceful | unpleasing |
| dismission | sending away |
| display | * what has ever been seen (as in "past display") |
| display, make | * look at or watch |
| dispose | [In *Hermes*, II. 330–31 "dispose Possessions to me" means "give me possessions"] |
| dispred | spread out |
| distinguished | separated |

# Glossary

| | |
|---|---|
| divine | make divine |
| divined | divine |
| doctrine | training, skill |
| drad | dread |
| ease | easing |
| eat | ate |
| egregious | noble, eminent |
| either | both (as in "either hand," meaning "both hands") |
| elaborate | * elaborating, adorning (as in "bestowing an elaborate hand") |
| empair | 1) impairment |
| | 2) hurt or damage |
| emperie | empire |
| employed | * brought to pass, caused to be |
| enamour | give delight or charm |
| encline | persuade |
| endless | immortal |
| enforce | produce by force, accomplish |
| ensue | follow or pursue |
| entertain | * answer |
| entreat | * address |
| equal | that is equal to ("equal Gods" means "Gods who are my equals") |
| err | wander |
| errant | wandering |
| event | [Used in various peculiar phrases: "dead event" is "death," "bear event of" is "be regarded as"] |
| evert | turn ("evert the good" means "turn the good aside") |
| everted | * sacked (of cities) |
| excitement | incitement |
| excogitate | think up |
| exempt | free from (as in "exempt from Pere," "exempt from match," which mean "peerless," "matchless") |
| exile | set apart or dismiss |
| exonerate | lighten |
| expert | free from |
| exploratorie | * exploring, searching (as in "exploratorie spirit") |
| explore | search |

# Glossary

| | |
|---|---|
| extuberance | something that swells up |
| eye | sight (as "in Apollo's eye") |
| fact | action, deed |
| facture | 1) the action of making a thing |
| | * 2) craft |
| fall | descent ("make a fall" means "descend" and "still pouring on their fall" is used of one army bearing down on another) |
| far-come | * far-comer, comer from afar |
| far-shot | far-shooting |
| fashionist | * one who follows current fashions |
| fautress | patroness |
| fenceful | * giving defence |
| fervent | * quick to burn (as applied to dry wood) |
| fescue | * plectrum |
| filed | 1) defiled |
| | 2) deceitful |
| fire-hov'd | fire-hoofed |
| fistularie | * ["Fistularie Reede" means a "pipe"] |
| fixed fight | battle |
| flame | * woman in love |
| flead | flayed |
| flit | * [Apparently in *The Fornace*, I. 25 this means "dust," according to the original πάντ' ἔντοσθ' αὐτῆι κεραμήια λεπτὰ ποιούσα] |
| flood | ["Ayre's flood" means "the air"] |
| floting | floating on |
| floure | 1) flower |
| | * 2) herbage (as in "greene floure," meaning "grass") |
| fluent | 1) river |
| | * 2) flowing or flaring (used for flames) |
| forc't | enforced, despoiled |
| fordge | forge (used in adjectival sense) |
| fore-right | straight forwards |
| forspoke | forespoke, bewitched |
| fortressing | turning into a fortress |
| free | set free or dismiss |

# Glossary

| | |
|---|---|
| fully-divin'de | completely divine |
| futurely | in the future |
| gable | cable (of a ship) |
| ghesse | guess |
| glory | 1) boasting |
| | 2) fame |
| gode | goad |
| grievance | sense of grief, terror |
| grought, growght | growth |
| guilt | gilt, gilded |
| gynn | gin, device, instrument |
| gyrlond | garland |
| hair | head of hair |
| hant | haunt, dwell on |
| hanting | haunting |
| harpsical | * kind of harp |
| heed | attention, observation |
| height | [Used peculiarly in phrases such as "to his utmost height," meaning "to the best of his ability"] |
| herd, in | * in line with |
| herehence | from this |
| heyring | heiring, being the heir of, coming from |
| hill-bred | bred on the hills |
| hollow | shout |
| honorarie | * honourable, worthy of honour |
| humorous | watery |
| humour | liquid |
| hurreys | * hurries, hastenings (of coaches) |
| ill-named | * called or styled ill |
| illude | cheat |
| illustrate | make to shine, glorify |
| immane | monstrous |
| immanitie | monstrous deed |
| imperatorie | * concerned with ruling ("imperatorie art" is the "art of government") |
| imply | * place (as in "did his point implie in") |

# Glossary

| | |
|---|---|
| impose | place, set, up or on |
| impression | * [Used in peculiar phrases such as "standing th' impression of the first in fight," meaning "getting the first shock of the onset"] |
| inaccessible | unreachable, unmatchable |
| indevirginate | * unravished, virgin |
| indifferencie | absence of bias |
| indifferencing | * impartial |
| inexcitable | from which one cannot be roused (as in "inexcitable sleepe") |
| infer | introduce, bring |
| inflexive | * inflexible |
| inform | 1) make, form out of, construct |
| | 2) Inspire |
| infortune | misfortune |
| ingenuities | * beauties, things of skill (as in "Poesie's ingenuities") |
| ingenuous | noble |
| inhabitresse | one who 'inhabits |
| innumerous | without number |
| inquest | question, finding out |
| insolent | strange, terrible |
| instauration | start, beginning |
| interest | matter of concern (as in "of interest in," meaning "concerned or associated with"; "your interest," meaning "things concerned with you") |
| invention, find the | invent |
| inveterate | old-standing |
| jack | buff jerkin |
| jarre | battle |
| jointly | at the same time |
| kind | nature, race (as in "fetcht his kinde from," meaning "was descended from") |
| kirnell | kernel |
| knoule | knoll |
| kymnel | tub |
| languor | grief |
| lay abroad | * debate |

# Glossary

| | |
|---|---|
| lengthful | lengthy |
| Lernean | * vile, monstrous |
| list | limit, check (as in "list or Lawe") |
| livrings | liver puddings |
| los'd | loosed |
| lurch | deceit |
| lust | will, desire |
| lybberd | leopard |
| lynce | lynx |
| man'de | maned, having a mane |
| mankind | fierce |
| manly | bold |
| manned | * occupied with (as in "mann'd with sheepe") |
| mastery | work of distinction |
| mere | simple, pure |
| mere-learn'd | learned men who have no other virtues |
| merit | * ["In merit of" means "because of, through"] |
| mind | * 1) knowledge ("uttered minde" is "speech") |
| | * 2) courage (as in "each Frogg full of Minde") |
| mind-master | * spirit of courage |
| miseries | * [In "Miseries to his Merite" the sense seems to be "miserable treatment" and hence "neglect of"] |
| moule | mole |
| murmur | noise |
| mutiny | warlike preparation |
| neese | Sneeze |
| next | that which was next |
| neye | neigh |
| note | benefit, use (in *Hermes*, I. 48 "Thou mov'st in me a note of excellent use" means "You are of benefit to me by showing how you can be put to good use") |
| numerous | rhythmical, musical |
| nursery | process of nursing |
| nutritial | * concerned with nursing or fostering |
| offspring | [Used in *Apollo*, I. 578 for animals sacrificed at the altar] |
| ope-war | open, or openly declared, war |
| opprobation | * impertinence (spelt "opprobation" in the original, but possibly intended for "opprobration") |

[223]

# Glossary

| | |
|---|---|
| opprobrie | condemnation, reproach |
| op'te | oped, opened |
| ostent | outward sign |
| oughly | ugly |
| ought | owed, owned |
| outray | * outgoing, expedition ("on all the Outraies where for food I erre" means "in all the expeditions when I wander about seeking food") |
| overture | * innermost part (of a cave) |
| owe | Own |
| past | paste |
| pecuniarie | * having to do with money ("pecuniarie Rates" means "commerce") |
| pedigree | race |
| penurie | lack, destitution |
| perdue | lying in ambush |
| pere | peer |
| perpendicular | * virtue |
| perspective | * sight, view |
| perspirable | * airy, hence lofty (as in "perspirable heights") |
| petulant | wanton, bold |
| phane | fane |
| plash | * plashed thicket |
| plume | * bird |
| plump | crowd |
| possest | possessed, demonic |
| prærupt | steep, precipitous |
| prease | press |
| preast | pressed |
| present | [In *Venus*, I. 463 "so well Present the Deities" means "be so god-like in appearance"] |
| prest | ready |
| prise | take as a prize |
| project | abandoned, abject, base |
| propension | inclination, tendency |
| proyning-<br>bank | * [This seems to mean a bank where a bird preens itself] |
| prime | first ("tooke Prime existence" means "was born") |

# Glossary

| | |
|---|---|
| purvaie | * take |
| queach | thicket |
| rac't | razed |
| raie | ray |
| rapting | ravishing |
| rapture | seizing away |
| ray | * vision, glance |
| receipt | * cave, cavern |
| receit | receipt |
| reciprocal | * one who is sent back (as in "You must be made your own Reciprocals to," meaning "You must be sent back") |
| recourse | [See under "convert"] |
| recreative | humorous, amusing |
| rector | chief |
| refulgency | * refulgence, glory |
| regency | act of ruling |
| relation | account |
| rely | [Perhaps in the dedicatory verses II. 53–54 "relies Refuge" means "reposes relief, or release"] |
| remove | * [Used peculiarly in such phrases as "in opposite removes," meaning "in reverse," and "thou put'st on Remove," meaning "you removed, or moved, over"] |
| repair | * return |
| repose | * [None of the usual senses fit "his heart within him panted out repose," apparently meaning simply "palpitated" (i.e., was agitated), and "in steep'st repose," which seems to mean "in the highest position"] |
| rer'de | reared |
| restriction | * transference |
| retire | cause to retire, conceal |
| retreatful | * acting as a retreat |
| retrive | retrieve |
| rigging | * trickery |
| rore | ["Wavie rore" means "roaring waves"] |
| rumour | word, report |
| sacring | consecrating |
| sail, bear no mean | * be base or inglorious |

| | |
|---|---|
| sais'd | seised, put in possession |
| sale-muse | * muse put out for sale |
| salve | explain away |
| saving | bringing safety or salvation |
| scath | scathe, hurt, damage |
| scruple | doubt, uncertainty |
| sease | seize |
| seed | child, offspring ("while the streame her fluent seede receives" evidently means "while the waters flow," translating ἔστ᾽ ἂν ὕδωρ τε νάη) |
| sensual | addicted to merely sensuous pleasures |
| sent | scent |
| set | 1) [In *Hermes*, I. 792 this seems to mean "playing" (of an instrument)] |
| | 2) sat |
| | 3) fixing |
| set-spleend | * set down with spleen |
| sever | 1) break up |
| | 2) bring a speech to an end |
| several | something belonging to an individual |
| sex-distinguish't | * of both sexes |
| sharp-seen | * seeing keenly |
| shew, in | in appearance |
| shrick't | shrieked |
| shrike | shriek |
| shroud | place of concealment, recess |
| sight | power of seeing |
| simplicity | sincerity |
| sincere | pure, unmixed |
| singular | * [In *Hermes*, I. 853 "aspires to singular" seems to mean "aims at singularity"] |
| skeane | dagger or sword |
| sleight | slight, device, trick |
| snew | snowed |
| solace | [See under "abode"] |
| sort | decree of fate |
| souc't | soused |
| spell | talk |

# Glossary

| | |
|---|---|
| spring | 1) race, progeny |
| | * 2) father, begetter |
| springal | youth |
| spritelie | sprightly |
| square | * law |
| state | [This seems to be used almost as "position" in "thy endanger'd State" and "an eternall state in his affection"] |
| stealth | stealing |
| stere | 1) stir |
| | 2) steer (as in *Batrachomyomachia*, I. 114 where the Greek has οὐρὴν μὲν προπέτασσεν ἐφ' ὕδασιν ἤυτε κώπην σύρων) |
| stern | rudder |
| sterved-like-ravenous | * rapacious, rapaciously |
| stick off | * set off |
| storm | bring upon violently |
| strain | family, descent |
| striving | competing with one another |
| submitted | ["Submitted to my seat" means "which he has given to me as my seat"] |
| sumpture | * splendour |
| supplies | help |
| supply | ["In supply of it" means "in its place"] |
| surrogate | deputy |
| sustain | ["Sustaining a retreat" is simply "retreating"] |
| swim | swimming, power of swimming |
| taint | touch |
| talents of justice | scales of justice |
| tapistries | * [In *Pan*, I. 25 this clearly means "hiding places"; the word may be formed from the verb "tapis" or "tapish"] |
| taught | made aware of |
| thirst | thirst for |
| throat | loud cry |
| tiller | part of a bow |
| transcension | carrying or driving over |

[227]

# Glossary

| | |
|---|---|
| transfer | throw, cast |
| treble | speak in a treble, whine |
| treen | belonging to trees |
| trim | manners, fashion, equipage |
| tumble | tumble or throw down |
| tutress | female instructor |
| unexcogitable | * unthinkable |
| universal | prevalent over all (in "his universall entrails" it simply means "all") |
| unpris'd | unpriced, priceless |
| useful | * use or luck bringing (translating ἐριούνιοι) |
| utmost | outermost |
| vaine | * [There seems no known sense of "vain" or "vein" which fits "t'advance a vaine," meaning "to lift or rise up"] |
| vanted | vaunted |
| vehicular | * provided with wheels |
| vent | * ["Giving vents of life and motion" means "killing"] |
| view, at | * in full sight ("to their view" is "to see them") |
| voluntary | a piece of music |
| weeds | garments |
| whirlpit | whirlpool |
| wishful | delightful |
| witherling | * twisted, emaciated creature |
| without | outside of |
| wiving | * ["Wiving conversations" means "ideas about marriage"] |
| wowe | woo |
| wreakful | full of vengeance |
| yrckesome | irksome |